INFINITY BLUES

BY RYAN ADAMS

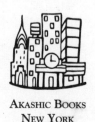

AKASHIC BOOKS
NEW YORK

Published by Akashic Books
©2009 Ryan Adams
Illustrations ©2009 Ryan Adams

Paperback ISBN-13: 978-1-933354-74-3
Paperback Library of Congress Control Number: 2008937347

Hardcover ISBN-13: 978-1-933354-83-5
Hardcover Library of Congress Control Number: 2008938820

Akashic Books
PO Box 1456
New York, NY 10009
info@akashicbooks.com
www.akashicbooks.com

The author would like to acknowledge the following people for inspiration or guidance, whether real or imagined:

Albert Einstein, Bug, Steve Martin and everyone at Nasty Little Man, David Letterman, Sheila Rogers, Paul Shaffer, and all at the *Late Show*, Jwlzy, Fire Party, Robert Thurman, Carl Sagan, Margaret Betts, Keith Morris, Stephen King, Jay-Z, Cameron Crowe, the Dalai Lama, Mary-Louise Parker, Amy Lombardi, Tony Dedmond and Hazel Dedmond, Nas, Michele Fleischli, John Silva, and the SAMily, Johnny Temple, Johanna Ingalls, Arielle Cohen, and everyone at Akashic Books, Mark Strand, Dawn Nepp, Josh Grier, Henry Rollins, Mac McCaughan, Brad Pemberton, Neal Casal, and the Cardinals family, Michael Panes, (   ), Voivod, the Boston Red Sox, and the cast and crew of *Moonlighting* (especially Cybill Shepherd who is eternally hot, like pancakes frying on the hood of a summer Honda).

Special thanks to comics, girls, and heavy metal (and/or punk rock).

for Bug

and for people who still read these things

Table of Contents

CHAPTER 3: INFINITY BLUES

CHAPTER 4: CHAPTER 11

CHAPTER 5: TOMORROW HAPPENS

Foreword

Once in a life, if a person chooses to go through these things, then maybe the act of writing them down could be a gift, so that others might know that should they suffer their romances or their love of things, they're not alone.

I no longer know the author of this book, for simply stopping long enough and writing it down was where I changed from a boy with his eyes squeezed shut to a man with his eyes wide open so that the sunlight might reach my heart despite all that darkness.

Go forward, be brave, and keep the faith.

Ryan Adams
October 2008

Firestorms Day One

Hot Georgia Damn,
i thought;
almost out loud over a blasting television—
mantle-mounted and crooked slightly;
a butterfly is laughing
wired-born without wings; color-wired
wired-shaky; riddled with desires and all that nothing to become—
in a row of blondes
lined up neck in neck
on a beaten couch
all of them soft as ice cream from a summer county fair
their faces interrupted not a touch
until wherever the last once sat
and the desk interrupted
the avenue breeze
grown calmed down from so far up the street
seeping into the window crack
all scooby-doo and shit
like a funky mist
but that was my heart going TICK TICK TICK
because
while they sat
and my friend drolled over each and every lap and leg
i saw a video
by that metal band RATT
where the guitar player crashes through the ceiling
to solo
on a proper dinner
in an upper-class flat
and i said,
"the only thing more punk would be if he stopped and asked,
'is that a de Kooning, you know, a real one and not a print?'"
like Harry Caray commenting on the Cubs
and i heard the most incredible laugh—
then
i saw a firestorm of slow curls
and eyes
the kind that send men packing
looking my way—
and i was now like
moons
moons crashing into each other—between my teeth

where there was supposed to be breath
and the dust
it just cracked
into a hopeless swarm of bad ideas
secret languages
and future amulettes
my god
i thought,
Hot Georgia Damn;
and
this is where we begin.

Home Safe—Heartsickness

home safe
just get home safe
heartsickness, my body said,
my body said stuff, it talked shit like a sewer rat eater
born in an orchid patch
glittering STOP signals
two
two of me watched
one down
two across
"l o n e l i n e s s"
only five letters, and too long
two words reach across the page of time
and
turn it into the reach of time
destroying this page

when the fixes are new losses
apologize
then get lost
kind of talk

i'd tell you i was so wrong
but how could i
if i stand in this fire
over and over
like
a bird begging for new beginnings
to cast more pain
unto itself
and shield the colors of sky
in
a sad mythology
of
southern export-style lies
riddled
with stains of honey
and
poison.

Babycakes

So,
while you were busy playing cards
I stole the snakes
from the suitcase
Did you win?
I bet you did
Either way you made your money back
Considering, you know
it's just cash you would have spent on me
and drinks
and mice poison
or mice
you know, more mice to feed the snakes
so maybe poison isn't right
and I meant more snacks
tossed over the pull-blanket
always in place
foot-side and glowing blue from movie burns
Now Listen Up,
babycakes . . .
Before the sun begins to rise
and that game goes stale
walk away
act natural
use your lipstick for blush if you hit the head and, you know
go all pale
and fidget-fingered
Before you crawl through the floor
carpet loud red and all
out the golden door
into the parking lot of our room
in that hotel
and find me gone . . .
I took the car
yes
But if you act fast you can catch the bus
to anywhere
but us
minus me and the snakes
and the magic
in the dust
good luck

babycakes,
may you always win
for thick claws
and soft skin
dry tears
out the window with my face
on the sky
and what is now left of the wind
the wind of gone.

Annihilator

I have nothing left to lose
and dream loosely before bed
after I take
a handful of prescribed medications for sleep
and over-the-counter vitamins
I think
"let me just die" but so quietly inside
with my quiet voice
and then tell that voice to hush
it is what is left of the ghost
I packed
and moved out of my body
on May 7th
with the help of a somebody (   )
annihilator
I have nothing left to lose
the love of my life
Blah Blah Blah I think when I write that
or Hollywood
I could go there
because it kills everyone equally
for the empty coast it fills faces pails
and like sailboats
on fire
in a mouth that will not smile
and a schedule
that cracks
water filling up a boat
nobody even looks at the plastic pales
water inside, water outside
endless "whatevers"
but who wants to die like that
   A newscaster loses it on live t.v.
starts screaming "fuck" over and over again
head in hands
"we are all going to die alone"
her wedding ring glistening
in the middle of a report on adopting kittens
and the closing of a kill shelter
in one of the boroughs
   then she says, "trust me"
and walks off the set

into consequence
red trees and faces melted safe
grandmother safe
like the lines of her face
safe
back to that
the honeymoon is over and I want to set this place on fire
something is wrong with me
annihilator.

To Flame

to flame
i am
so moth
to sing
i am
so lost
to lose
i am
so win
so where do we begin?
no time for stories
evictions
on birthdays
uptown/downtown
like a job for the sickness inside i have left to rob myself from
any good work
actually
i am not sleeping again
K.O.ed
evening declines
and another break-up
despite
the echo of "please, not now"
this is the finale
the wind-up
the blow-off
the pay-up
what the shoemaker threw at his wife
fat basket case of nerves
hair falling out
alpha-omega-terminate
the crack of doom
the close
last dollar shoved into a sock
the shutdown
the knockout of an infection
that lessens the pain
as you drift in a hospital bed
into extinction
no new beginnings
to flame
i am

so moth
to sing
i am
so lost
so lost
to flame

Time Ain't Nobody's Friend

Without the dress
she is so empty she sees
only empty showers with no soap
and no hot water
in a hotel room
her saints immediately become whatever available t.v. personalities
available
or maybe
street people
visible
through the disgusting curtains
either way
time is nobody's friend
you get
ten kisses, the kind in the air
if the air were your cheek
and your face were a balloon
a bag of air
fuck if i care, seriously
the idiot will stop us
from saying any of this
all that shit on the street
that junk, headboards and bedroom stuff
cars blazing past it on the street
time is nobody's friend
i am sick
in the head
all i wish
is to see you in the morning again
and this
this would all be a bad dream
in a series
Stephen King would be proud of
but
last things first
first rattle out of the box
it's time to open presents
i got a rattlesnake with ratios and equivalents
headlines
to break ice
ice-breaker goes for his coat
and opens fire

and my chest explodes in blood and guts
plus thimbles next
you can't sow back the seeds inside me of bad trees growing bad things
to throw away against your own personality
full-on spring, smelling like a rat
all broken into lies and things to throw out
without thinking
like a vanishing point—reappearing again
and again
time ain't nobody's friend.

For My Father, the Drunk

When I shave I save the mustache
for last
it reminds me of my dad
and I wish I had a dagger
I would put it in my chest
this is the place
he would not feel it best
for my heart
it is his
as he held me back
when my mother's hand broke the glass
through the door
to grab my shirt
and try and kill me some more
when I moan about things I cannot change
and all that money
that I could have saved
but spent
killing her pain
THAT is my mother's wish
I tuck myself into bed
but
I will never rest
she turned me into a shark
maybe from the poison
and roaches
that crawled over my brother's face
in housing
unfit for children
where someone got raped
raped
and beaten
black and so blue
no love even now at 33 will ever get through
with the words as a shield
and a metal vest
this is the place where I feel best
paranoid
and hopeless
I take my pills for days
I take my pills for days
I was a nightmare dreams could never save

poor girls who tried
become saints
in a book I bind with my veins
one sunday
this will pass
but not go away
screaming my way out from the ass-end of bars
I was back then nothing but scars
but for my father,
the drunk,
who married a stripper when I was five
I hope you close your eyes peacefully
and die

i shot the lights out too

i shot the lights out
on a million girls
when i should have stayed
balancing things
i could not save
born coward, taught slave
to be a fool
nourished on fears
and afraid
no if and or all these things
no arms
will ever be big enough to hold me
afraid of beds
and sex
and what it might mean
people
they are the strangest things
BUT
i am sort of saying thank you right now
saying,
ok, i surrender these things
i give in
mouth watering—thirsty but not swallowing
curves with incentive
and never coming through
all because of me
and my ways
there are a million-plus-sixteen guys out there
better
than me, kid
and all of them for you
i am lying alone
in a castle of bones
under a blanket
time to go
close the door
and leave because i have only the one shot left
and i shot the lights out
already
and this last one
it is not for me
and not for you

but for
a silence
and
none of god's business

Million-Year Fuck-Face Convention

How old you have become
how old
how frail
how made of things you used to hate
and wished you didn't feel

turns on the water
stands in front of mirror
the day (or what's left of it)
impatiently waiting outside the door

one more swallow of beach-water
something to remind me of mother
drowning me or my brother
in dirty bathwater
like that
I am holding my breath
in a sigh
of a sweet long goodbye
black-and-white movie style

burning all the leaves in the yard
in piles
in a thanksgiving card
signed
in paper-cut blood
and
it smells like cheap roses
and says,
"I thought you might like to see a picture of a home"
and not signed
because it was written
by a hag
who pushed me out
in a hospital
people drive a county away to
when they are missing a leg
gin-drunk and xanaxed to a couch
in a hole
cheap rose perfume
spitting in my face, on my soul
fuck you

red to green
red to green
I run so fast I run so fast I run so fast
I run so fast
I run so hard
you won
I am unfit to love
your revenge on your ex-husband my dad is complete
I resign
in defeat
stop stabbing me
and
stop staring
I will not be signing anything
at the million-year fuck-face convention

SOS Searchlights

it's too late to beg
she is not coming back again
and she was everything
everything
i ever saw, too perfect for words
i prepare a knife
and barricade the door
but she will not miss me when i am gone
and she is not coming back again
so what for
it is more painful
to sit here in silence
and suffer
the searchlights are off
the search has been called
i am drifting now
into dark
things nibbling at my toes
while the ocean
rolls my bones
like dice
on a wall of jokes

i wish i could say, "meet me at home"
it used to be mine or ours
how strong is a love?
not that strong
i tell my insides
as they churn for food or something awful and loud
oh god
no sleeping dogs lie
if it breaks
like a violin bowed to death
numbers
to protect the innocent you change the names
so i will change my address
and leave the rest the same
and how time does pass
when you slowly go insane from pissing up your rope
in your head
pretending
you are still lying on her stomach

listening to her laugh
as the radio goes BLRGHHH
both windows shut
and the door to the bedroom closed
in a touch
i dream we race each other home
progress documented by cell phone
but i don't live there anymore
your heart
hours hover over me as the glacier collapses
into the sea
home—safe
but now you
are the medication i repeat
my medication repeats
and
my mind retreats
but
it's over
and
my money goes to old fucking men in chairs uptown
married for twenty years
who lie to me
and say,
"one day you will laugh"
and
I sit and smile back like I am supposed to
and
plan another death
as
i drift
into a night
and
just wade
like food
not even
dark things under me would eat
for
the curses inside
and
god
with his timing
and rods
of lightning
tuned

to
my hopeless desires
it's too late

Night of Bones

Once there was a boy lonely as a night of bones. Bones in a box. Box in the ground. Once there was a world so full of light and so full of darkness, it seemed impossible to know what was what, and in the shade of the light he rested. This was his way. His flow.

Flow was and is everything.

Night shattered the glass. He wasn't sure if his hand just seized or the muscles froze because he had made them and did not know, but the glass, it shattered across the floor till it was smaller than a handful of earrings. These evenings had begun and did not seem to stop. They had crept up on him like a progression of bad dreams, like a series of drones. And it was important to keep people around now that he was so alone.

The calmest and scariest place was in the bath, covered in suds, listening to his radio. In his thoughts the past would dwell like hanging ghosts. Plants talked. Unicorns existed in the history museum. Ancient texts were all hidden truths of the world unexposed. He was sick. Like a blue dog. Like an ice trunk on a private yacht.

Blue Wars

Part I.
the cars up on the lake
I'm only joking
there is no lake
only a street
and on this street
we live alone
I have a room
I keep a picture
by my bed
of the war
I need to talk and not with my mouth
I need to feel and not with my felt
I need some security
fuck
my youth is over
the ending is coming
all the stars are burning out
not growing
but idiots with guitars are strumming
I am one of them
and I am awful
out of tune since yesterday
as if it was the 1800s
and
as much as I would like to be in love
I am not
punk is dead
and my best friend says,
"oh well, let's fuck"
and
I just, you know, puke—throw up
what's more important—
first kiss or last?
you have to know these things nowadays
because
it will not end well—
and that is how we are taught
latch-key mall rat from the '80s or not
I wrote a melody once
in an elevator at 6 a.m. for booze
and prospects

i got scars and civil war artifacts
and clues
bar napkins stuffed into my pockets
scratched into them like they were arms
and I was a cutter with terrible blues
from blue wars
there is part two.

Oblivion

You know what they say,
If the show fits . . .
Well it fit you, it had to have
You bought the whole store

Playing games with the boys in the bar
Telling your version of the story
Saying it loud enough that anyone listening
can hear the new edition you revised
to attract them

Lies Lies Lies
with X's on the eyes
You're a company in trouble
miserable and downsized
Lies Lies Lies
busy-bodied slacker
who's a slacker attracter
Starcrossed,
and only lucky with the lazy ones.

You know what they do,
get drunk on information
then they actually get drunk
and tell anyone who'll listen

You're getting good at this
Good work, keep up the practice
One day you'll be above them all
and I'll be fine, I got a cactus

Lies Lies Lies
Put X's on their eyes
Your company's in trouble
You're miserable since you were downsized
Lies Lies Lies
Shoving boys into the bags
that you emptied out your shopping in
You're starcrossed and lucky
with all the lazy ones   What's
another name for slacker, it's a bum
idiot starfuckers

Sign your name in the space above
don't call her
she'll call you
You can audition for her love.
Just remember
she's only lucky with the lazy ones
Go mess up your hair
lose the tie and stand right here
you're on.

What Is the Password for Summer Again?

Birthday Gemini
stares back at the glasses through bright candle glow
stares through the plate
a pill went down
probably
it says it all
says, "for now, this night is too late"
with no waterfall
no father-and-son type dialogue
stupid like a flock of rackety glisteners
champagned and smiling
like geese
some asshole talks about poetry
and
you know,
she sleeps with him
so gross
not even cheap
just fucking gross, and wasted on the sheets
who am i to be the one to tell him who
or what
when i am just a thought
in a flying spitball
not even a contender
on a flight
of nobility
barely an example of either gender
inside soft like pound cake and sweet tea
a world of vessels
with me a dam
that would never let a single fucking boat come in
without firing on it
before a warning sound or shot
i am a war
—she sits and stares and watches
sits and stares and wastes her time
like I am not looking
red hair like bloody morning
cars begin
and interrupts the happening
and
if it was true, ever, anything inside

then
the weight of love should crush us both
like summer bugs
but
separated forever
without the password for summer
just outside
for my bones ache for you
like i was not here
yet
and a season to forget
i am only a word slut

Snow Lady, I Wished You

sweet dreams,
snow lady
cinderella shoes
and tap
tap
tap
on the walls

my eyeballs fall out
I cry
during funny parts
of *ghostbusters*
now
I am old

it's so funny
you would even laugh
sociopath

and I guess I don't belong to you
than I do the South anymore
dodo bird
wasted moment
crashed car
traffic accident
real
heartbreaker

it was nice to meet you
i think

sweet dreams
for
every day that finishes you in bright light
and
honestly
may you sleep so sound
and
live eternal in my heart
as
an amulette
made of something stronger than hope

snow lady

Gay As Fuck

write a line
cross it out
nothing i say
is ever good enough
anyway
my stomach is turning
bloody gray
full of rust
riddled with cliché
and gay as fuck

dirt in my room
vacuumed to death
until the curtains
get sucked
until night's only left
night is only left for me to piss off
riddled with envy
and gay as fuck
dreaming impossible girls
who spit and cuss
on car windshields
pulling out guns
and firing at famous cemetery headstones
in gingham dresses
and
with busted lips
the leaves go red
orange and brown
a tree gets chainsawed
tree falls down
falls on the fence
of the house that I bought
for us
my life is a comedy
i am a hack
and this is just nothing
and
gay as fuck
sarcastically
with
a Southern accent

in the back of mind
Auden's complete works
held up
to God
as light
of course
still,
gay as fuck
as if to say
so
what.

You Will Not Miss Me When I Am Gone

Car goes past
the window in the room
the lamp by the bed burned out last night
and it's almost afternoon
seashore lined with bars
Broadway girls missing
into the mouth of the moon
mid-autumn
and you will not miss me when i am gone
Heaven and Earth
Body and Soul
last light of day
flowers in the cold
sand and sea
how happy we used to be
memory
oh you
two tickets for the movies
foolishly bought in line
one stub
just me
I do this shit all the time
think for two
on my sea-lined shore of fake bars
with fake lights and fake nights
and fake drunks with fake drunk fights
there are holes in my wallet pocket
from where my lonely chair rubs
as I write nothing
but alibis
and you will not miss this when i am gone
things
they might have been different
had we a map
anyone's
but I am not going back to the airport like that
even if you died first
which you won't
unless there is some sick sense of humor left
in a universe of irony
because
to you I am certainly dead already, lover

at least
those stars
shine from someplace beyond
maybe I can go
but
I leave with my head hung as low as a gong
for now
for you are strong
and weighted to the ground
and
you will not miss me when i am gone
the million years
it took
to become starfigures
weight-measures
and moon
dissolve
in cups of solitude
bad poetry and cash registers
collapsing into a taxi door closed and moving
slow down
I came all this way
he
he closes his eyes and drinks her
as if in prayer
the spirits come take him and
she is more than that
I throw a pillow across the room
and
fucking
scream
this is destroying me
not him
but to her somewhere
as if in a dream
sign the receipt
go home
it's 4

and i have had enough, my dear, for both lifetimes
so
so
so
sorry
fuck

Elf Mountain

. . . Elf Mountain,
i rely on you
and a soft gang of unicorns
plus
the medicine
to help me find that strange thing—
that strange valley
      sleep
i find it so hard to imagine
      or reach
. . . Elf Mountain,
do you have a favorite
set of marbles in your
jar of brains
of things to help you
do "that" but something
      opposite
of me when i am awake
      like this?
      I bet
—suppose we dreamed some people up
  just like ourselves and here and
  now, as i write or you read,
made them, you know . . .
fit and freckled
or
you know, whatever tickled your belly
or my belly, you know, like whatever
really and we just
set them free
like you would
a butterfly
    no seriously
if it landed in the palm of your hand
i know someone
    you
that this once happened to
    and
with a smirk and a mouth full of teeth
and bad ideas and godknowswhat mischief
    and crushed it
like a bug with wings

crushed it
its living colors dying
fluorescent bloody wings
      oozing guts
      green with
somebody, somebody so beautiful just laughing
   like in a face,
beyond god if god were a figure standing
      behind him a thousand shielded angels
      with swords
ready to engage the wicked
. . . Elf Mountain
you know, she and i barely spoke
so it never came up
she and i, we kept it
juvenile and crass
like our lives, and that, that romance
was like smoking cigarettes on the fire escape
a metaphor of our lives
in the cold
of winter
always
. . . Elf Mountain,
i was admiring your flying machine, that blanket
with satin at the edges of it,
a little worn for the worse
you have a favorite, see we all do
maybe you build them at night
like i do
helpless against dreams
and silence
which to me
sounds like screams or madness or something
wicked this way always coming
always
smoking cigarettes on the fire escape
his cloak
glowing
and rushing to kill me
so i am riddled with that natural
or unnatural fight
against it
but your hand so freely reaches for the light
and you dine on your peace
as a swallow of water should

but my
body and soul
just say no
naturally to that place of letting it all go
even though,
Elf Mountain,
it is THOSE quiet places i rely on
so if
i should happen past her on a street
my eyes will be as blank
as
all the lies that it has
sweated in a kitchen to make
so poison pie
may clog the lake
and flood us all
inside my face
the thinnest walls of a skin
versus a time, time winning
always scientifically
smoking cigarettes on the fire escape
in the always winter
i rely on dreams
and the medicine
or die
Elf Mountain, and you
you

A Death

i feel a Dying in me.
a death
like my inside cat knows
like,
It eyes the door
and i am not
not helping
        today i held the door like a gentleman
        yes sometimes for real sometimes pretend
        who looked up at me
        from her winter hat
White Eye, one
and the other
its gaze straight through me into infinity
beyond blues
laughed
she wheezed a healthy laugh this woman
as i hovered round the cash register
and i swear
she acted like
a death
        i had a handful of dvds on the Dalai Lama
    she asked me what they were i said "movie tapes"
        or she said "oh those are those movie tapes
    that go inside the television box"
    how ancient
she smiled
and it scared the man who rang up my things
i paid in cash, which is also ancient
and it was like he had forgotten what that was
stared but tried not
at that woman
that woman
a death
on rollerskates so to speak
eyes like the devil
ancient and evil
for the seeing of the littleness of an everything
fuck her, i thought
i see the balance
and i choose the light
into the sun and never a night

wins against my lonely
insides
grizzly bear hibernation lonely
but full of wonder
books
stacked where a woman goes
if she were to find my bed
hidden now from even me
location protected
by geography
and time
still
my toes do not stop their locking
and that pain
like my body knows
a death
still
my knuckles and toes
do their ghostly locking and unlocking
up and down
my legs and arms
my body
so quiet
creaks like a door
in a ghost house
and that pain
like
i feel a dying in me
a death
but seriously
so
fucking
what
whatever
right?
ha

One Sharp Ending

the natural law says no
that's what
that is why your eyeballs hurt
when you think of dying
why they blur from printed skirts
and static
why your chest heaves as she goes
into what
that pain is now
not her
but you
and your feelings, mister
it is like a jewel within your brow
your brain only a machine with legs
now
made of butterscotch minus drinks
and cigarettes
and loose tears
falling into neighbors' sinks
body upright
head, over and down
hair everywhere
over your nose
as you sniffle out the rose
and let in the air
no letters home from italy or somewhere
haunts you like a flu
in a flu hotel
that girl does
it is why you were born, reader
to fall in love
over and over
to die again
and push pain over
on its side
so the stories will spill out
war stories
about your mother and father
and nazis
scumbags, all of them
like children bent bad
playing follow-the-leader

listening to the sound of their own roar
the lighting of the churches
follows the ceremony of madness
that world
was burned to the fucking ground
blown straight to hell
for the making of new evil empires
or a mid-game Christ rebound
half-court shot
nobody knows really, only time will tell
either way
do this, if only for me please
redeem the powers of the gods
somehow
you can look at that part in her dress
where the shadow moves like a golden cat
undercover
in a strawberry mess
and
you could get busy dying in that
however many tiny deaths
it takes
to make your eyes roll back
or
if you let it pass
if she liked you
and
you give her a chance to undress
or she undresses you first
it would flow
out the sides
those stories of her fathers or mothers
through your mouth and insides
could root
or seed
and if it rained, which it will
it would let the growing come
up a city block of grainrows of you and her
to repeat
that doom
that cycle of living and dying
for every child brought into a hospital room
has no idea
there is a leaving to be done too
so cruel

Man
a monkey with a stick
with
one crushed handle
from bludgeoning skulls
and the other
thinned to a point
by nature
with
one sharp ending.

52 Pieces

silence
broke you
into 52 pieces
while
i watched
i saw you
you
you were en route to buy wine
you
you were leaving
somewhere
already
and i
i think i liked that
and
i think you knew
you
you knew i would rip open the air
and
make a space
large enough
large enough
for two
so
you could go through
because
i am always going through anyway
like
changing my destiny every hour
time travel
easy
is the same thing
same thing
as if i delivered pizzas
no bike
and
those portals are my version of the subway
which i dislike
my version of public transportation
is sitting still
and waiting for new clicks
on the wheel

of time
and
also
i saw you smile
and
i thought i could catch that in a jar
like you were a lightning bug
and
you knew i had holes poked in the top
from a flat head
pressure drop
me with my can full of holes
for a head
and
the glass was as deep
with me
and
the glass was as thin
as the idea
of
a fluttering of wings
easily shattering
offering
some release
as thin
as the idea of where
where my bedroom door closed
and
where my bed began
and this
this
this is our story
for now

A Sister Scowls

a sister scowls
at the monster
she knows
she knows
it has arms and legs like a spider
and a stinger
boxed with booksmarts
plus poison
fucking monster she sees
in a form
of family
and YOU know
and she knows
and
a sister scowls
    a red overcoat protects her skin
    under a sweater you gave her
you got from somebody
from letting someone in
into, you know
the kingdom,
blah, or yuck
your mother's daughter, she is
your mother's jewel
your father's memory
of stilts
and heels
and wheels
and bells
and observations of machine-gun fire in a belly
surrounded by nazis
one of them
maybe from up North
maybe who made a mother
out of us all
us children
later
a delicious woman who likes pasta
and gin gimlets and artist fodder
but sometimes with boys
my dear,
your memory fails

your baby-fat face with eyes low
under the fire of some mythological color
i so desperately desired
a halo and a heart
in the form of a fire
no gasoline tanker could start
for its cargo and shell
felled
like trees clogging the drain
in a sink if it were a well
of bad ideas gone wishes
and
nobody left to tell
you
a wildflower blowing a breeze blown round
party to party
endlessly
endlessly nobody
collecting personality confetti
after-hours
before the floors are swept
for good
matching colors your designs allowed you
entrance
with a face
and an accent
like that
whatever that is, that day, anyway
somewhere
your father lurks
a chamber of bones
his mouth
bloated germanic snob loud
and screaming at the monster
on a tiny pink telephone
with his stuffed rash bark
that dog
that useless patchy fog
of half ideas
on a loudmouth answering things
no one person might ever resolve
oh god
blah, and yuck
  and YOU know
  and she knows

and you will never cry
for a time before a sound
tells you
why
and
how
for a thought hits under your heels
and smashes to the ground
underneath the wheels
of my rig
full of cock and hope
and eventual betrayal
and you know
and she knows
and I did not
but she is full of fear
which makes me hot
because you scare us all
and she gives or gave me hugs
with every ounce
of an arm
she got
from your mother's lovely make
and skeleton gift
and
her name is genuine
as her gaze
in THIS dimension
    nervously she laughs
    all of us
    aware
of a why
a when
and a how
but still
  she knows
  she knows
and in your direction
unaware
at the monster
a sister scowls.

Rain on America

so dirty
so dirty and so mean
is a rainbow
is a letter-stained
is a blowhole sewer
that's right
just a touch of little america
in a small town
wishing you were gay
or allergic
to something
anything
symmetrical lines ripe with train machines
like arms
branches of trees stuck to this rock
out-stretching
blowing up fast
through
shadow mole-holes
and
rain
rain rain rain
so dirty
so dirty and mean
hands like a battling machine
like a failed robotic attempt
like an interruption at the movies
like texting your former lover
or future
because he will not stop your nevers
not here
with a little touch of america
at your service door
flags in the yard
dogs in the house
his name above
loose and no growl
little ones go teary and cross
while the plate gets heavy with
cigarettes and lip gloss
and gin-scum breath
and cigarette-tray stains

and a hand gets bit by an animal
but nobody screams
or says anything
the mall dies
so eventually
store by store
the zombies outside they aren't scary anymore
before the movies went cold before before
and the film backed up on the shilling and trade post
and chicken meat got hormonal and plain
so dirty
so dirty and so mean
little and loud
angry
and effortlessly proud
of nothing
and plain
just a little touch of america
rain
rain rain rain.

Becausewhy

because we are bored
We War
Because we are bored
We Fuck
sexy or not
and
Because we were born to fight
inside
we know
our children too, eventually will die
this is how it is
in the universe of ours
us against time
and
in this place,
show me where god stood up
and said otherwise
i say he does not speak
and may be everything
inside that thought
you are allowed
but may not keep
for the growing
of things
immeasurable
i have not seen him
while i have been alive
and regardless
heaven
that would not work
if men and women
were anything like this
someplace else
especially an elsewhere
of brights
and
if so
that is not a good place to go
i would not dine there
how could one relax
infinitely
in a place like that

so why?
becausewhy
that's what
that's what they say
right before
"shut up"
and i'm like
ok
no
never.
Fuck-Face.

Sisters

        two of them
        sisters
one of them
my lover
t.v. on stutter
news on gray
room aged white
windows half open
early,
but night
        two of them
        sisters
one of them
my lover
both of them
i like
i like
they look at funny pictures
inside fashion magazines
while people say the world
it is dying
i think it is
i think a lot
i think it might
don't sigh
i had a panic attack, then tea
there were these monsters
just outside of me
in this place, this rotten hole
of a face
a church mouse wouldn't enter
even bother
to remember
crossed
like a crucifix lost
or an open-backed dress
you buy at cost
i feel calm
around them
early,
but night
hotel room bed

bathed in the pillow-fight
not happening
nice blanket
unusually nice
    sisters
    two of them
one of them my lover
two of them
i like
i like

Electric Blue

Electric Blue light, right outside,
makes audible light, noisy-like
i think of nada
clear
like imagining everything before it emerged
from the deep
it's all new
my eyes are having a birthday party
happiness is invited
c'mon down
my lens are stuck and what,
what is this color?
Electric Blue Audible Orb
something
as if i mean to say, "the sky outside,
and the buildings, they're being born now, ok?"
before my very soul
and i
i would weep if it weren't for the joy or say
lack of water in the well, where
i buried myself again today
in those stupid sorrows
your memories, are they worth even a dollar
in pennies
you count, you're good at that
Amulette
your house is the spinner
brown
tornado
pulling up trucks and telephone poles
in the cotton-swell of rows of corn
like danglings
and you
you stick me inside that place
that bomb shelter
and tell me i am safe
i am NOT
but in you i know a terrible truth
the colors and a texture
like a strawberry sundae
cool pink and glass
and melting all over the place

only thing missing—polka dots
and
a few books on outer space
i saved some just in case
thank god
on the day we said goodbye to you and saluted the sea
no one
a casket slipping into the ocean like Elvis
a mystery
made of dream-silk
and spiders' eyes
that see everything to better invade a space
that your quiet punishment coughs go loudly in
and
it was as if you were lost at sea
and
god, even a few of my guy friends wept
seriously
what the fuck
what are you, a magician
is that your disappearing act?
my insides
become my outsides
so yuck
and are asked to leave
these numbers next to the words they go nicely like they're told
they go well with all this red, this book-binder and pen
fitting nicely in my front pocket
and your umbrella matched
no hood this time
just a heeled foot
a scarf and some gloves
and
my knees riddled with knicksandknacks from thisandthat
but puddle-water happy
jumping
and
rain-come-down wanting
sigh
i will sit here forever, me, just wondering why
watching
each pulse ripple from my neck vein on sheets
whimpering
like it was forever
for a second

on repeat
BUT
this is not pain
like
that was not love
like
this is all new
like
either way i am set free
and
like an animal
under the harsh globe metal-armed light
i get sewn back up
insides intact
but no anesthetic
eyes put back in
paws lifted
trying to understand english all of a sudden
how is this so
is this Electric-Rodeo Accident sky?
letting the puddles be the color i make
when i mix orange and white
plus gloss and clouds
if clouds are around
to be stuck in my paint's muck
how?
how is this so?
my god
my soul will surely explode
i am going to run my hand up the side of that pillar
like it was a sweaty-day leg under a fake yellow sun
and your back
was just lifted up against the bark
and from your knee
to the middle of your thigh
i have hands
big ones
Idea-sized

that fucking pillar has to be crazy tall
glowing gray
also with a halo
and rain-shatter wind-spray dribble
singular then plural
if i could, i would

undo that sky's dress
one shoulder strap at a time
and
mouth the words
to
the longest song
tune cracked
till it fell apart
into a pool of pink dots
faint
from come
and something a little louder than prayer
my
fucking
word
oh my

Dreamlines for Critics

Could ever a line cover this face; if we are the dreamers, dear reader
could it, i don't know, it's fun to say, say it out loud and clearly and let it go
like a hand releasing something alive
like a telephone call ending
like a design flaw
could a line cover this; we need answers; we need people on this
wood-paneled desks; cheap and with good typewriters; coffee
a few eccentrics and their cigarettes and someone, a drinker with no aftermints—
capable;
that is what
like an office to sort through this—
because
if we are reading poetry together now then one of us is amiss
and lost sort of, or looking;
because all that life is on the other side of the word
though the word
how much concrete is it really
right
how much weight on your back
right
and that flight of stairs outside every time
god it changes
it changes
it changes
people might not understand that from far away
we might all look like alley cats
even when we wear our best
expensive coat and vest
too tired in places, we might look
to someone
far outside this field
of the word
its lights burning up dark mellowing spaces in the overbite of entrances and
exits
or be they the same
you know
it's all a bit "coming" and "going"
if you have no place really
you were going
and
from a small window atop it all
it just looks like little flakes

street snowing
with faces
or
too many ants going too many places
could a line ever cover this;
i wonder
but not really
because
it is all here before us, dear reader, in the word
we find the balance
and the bird
and the string to its claw
and its message
if it is a falcon
if it is a carrier pigeon
stalled
and
like all of them
it might
just
end up belly-up in a fountain
and
there is always a woman crying on these streets alone hurrying home
at least
if you keep your eyes open long enough
and
have the stomach for it
to see
and no line could cover that or her
but a homemade quilt and some kind of corner-store dessert
because
soon
those tears go wilder than that and a face is a drowning place
and
something in the dream has given way while the dreamer
was half sleeping
and half living all awake
but
letting it happen anyway
right
right?
I don't know either, but
either way
Can a line ever cover this; if that is the question we need a crew, a team, a mass
of engineers

worthy of the pursuit of the mystery
of the origin of tears
because
it goes back before
the boy or girl
and the broken vase or plate
or the screaming
or the other person inside their clothes
when they might have been
at their friend's house
that afternoon
long before
long before
the being born
that sadness is an ancient thing, an aged storm
a reminder maybe
really, only
and
something inside you is a clock that is ticking in a color map and a feeling number
to count the things
that
lift you up and
drag you under
for
the swells of air if air were water
and
a line cannot cover this
so
no more lines
no more lines
no more lines
no more waiting
no more crying
no
not if you would like to return to the base you built on a hillside in your name
in your soul
because the sun is shining there
and the scary part
is really
the packing and getting ready to go
because
once you are done
and the sheets are soaked
and the mouth is shut
and

you are there with your bags in hand and a motion is about
to set in, you are in charge
of your body
and your things
and
you know
willing
that is where the next step begins
and
if we are dreamers
a line must cover what a line could never cover because
because
when they go,
and they are gone for good,
as are you,
a line is all we have
and
all that's left
so
get busy dreaming on the line dreamer
and
i will meet you in the after
if
it lets us
have a say
and
we will collect those lines together
maybe
even
forever

Taxi after Taxi . . .

Taxi after Taxi, I found the horrors; eventual and coming; with a dress; with shoes. Chrysler Building refracting mirrored balls of total madness; the throat choke ten paces from tears, and my face, just the face of a man with new losses to count. This was how it was. This was how it was meant to be. That is what they say to you, your friends, right when the shit is fresh upon the fan, "what will be . . ." But the colors of an overcoat and the sound of a voice and what fall and winter will mean feel almost as though a storm is on the face of the mountain and exhausted, you are resting in a foot-hold and your gloved hands are stiffening anyway inside the gloves, as the rope swings like a pendulum under new phone numbers to be cut, with a waiting madman below, rubbing his hands together like right before dinner, and you know two things: you are about to fall, and that man below is you.
Is this what a heart ache is?
No.
This is what it means to find the wall.
For every one worth any kiss would surely break them all, if you lined them up, like bowling balls
and gave THAT ONE the heavylight blue marble ball with the three holes.
One for each finger, not counting the thumb.
PRAY FOR A STRIKE
1. Whoever he is, be he now or next, he is better than you.
2. Reduce the amount of shoes you wear to only one pair; looking down will be new to you so steadily.
3. Pray for tears and might, because they will come for you, in the middle of the afternoon when her feet do not, and,
not to sound redundant,
but
Taxi after Taxi, we all know the horrors of the night;
the phone numbers that will not be yours and be his or theirs, you will not speak through,
there is a party somewhere and they are not focusing on you—and do not hear sobbing
for music and the possibility.
My God, where is this and why; this is what I think or what I thought as I watched this last storm go by and destroy the house, for its windows to the garden looking out, the other side, shrouded in a swarm of doubt around the trees we planted too fast and too suddenly and this is how it goes, and this is how it was meant to be.
But in these moments, when a lover leaves, you would like very much the wrench and the blueprints
of Destiny,
not the hooker Destiny or the dancer you met at the screening of a comedy, a

stage a theater on a street midtown where people do not live, or if they live
there you have never met those people for they live in the heart of the sun of a
city built by people caving in with math, making everything a grid—
so Taxi by Taxi—
one may move without a map.
But you always, or we always like to say the names, the corners, and their
complexity may vary in degree or range, but you like to say the names, they are
your landmarks,
and now
you may move without a map
you may lie upon the floor in tears and cry for nothingness
you may read a book, no watch
you may sleep in, maybe twice or not
you may stay awake and shake and examine dusty corners
you may pretend they have meanings unintended and
maybe you just were not looking before
was that there
is that a sign
when did that little cloth heart get a push pin next to a window
with
a crystal on a hook a suction cup and the light particles dance as they break up
like an outmoded satellite
you have been programmed now
to
reenter the atmosphere
and
become elemental, now
IF
if you surrender like a man does, when he would like to surrender the way
he believes a woman does, when he is a man like myself, and thinks only true
surrender has been witnessed or seen in crucifix—
through the blood and the wood and the nails, hung up on a wall or a hill,
regardless, sacrificed everywhere
. . . that kind of surrender that keeps you from getting there.
a. one pair of shoes for the walking one will need to do
b. the icons of the ages must fall so you may examine carefully and without
thought
WHEN
when she comes, if you are ready, when she comes, she does the very thing they
all did to you before
BUT when you are ripe and the tree is fit for fruit with questions inside its juicy
silk,
when you are almost at tilt,
that is when, unlike the others, you go small as a danger, small as a swallowing
then, bam

Cave-In

this is interrupted by the longest silence that no words could cover, no diagram
nor map.
You
it is only you now
and the pause.
Hold onto yourself as tightly as you can and cut the rope
and enter
enter into this fire, and pass through, because it only takes once
that one time
and then you understand desire,
and you
you just know, you just know who you are.
NOW
you may move without a map,
because we all know the horrors; pretty shoes and madness
and they are coming
Taxi by Taxi.

Perfect/Seasons

this season
i got it perfect again
understand that
perfect
like the woman says to the man
she will not let in again
"see you soon"
that is what i say to this season
so isolated
my harvest in
winter on steel and steel on tread
boots on feet
instead of sled
this concrete has a mark made
by the hand
twitchy
from the coffee and the slight grin
turned like a cat's
on the face of a kid
undone undid
this season
i got it perfect again
understand that
shouting
get your rooftop ready and your face
pressed into a wall and a
glass and an aspirin
get ready for summer
withdrawal
like there wasn't any hot
above me
angels rear heavy swords inside them stars
ready to swing
this season
perfect

The Break Bell

these old songs are the break bell
and the lanterns relighting
celebrations happen here
inside this
my love, at 26
feasts on bloody meat
and cocktail shimmy
for glass root
bath salt skin in a rush
with scrubbing gloves
and loves to dish
   a manhattan boat on stilts
water just tarmac and taxi smear
i was like, never here, or something
i bet,
they say,
to her,
when she just so parts her legs
and the line reveals infinite class
forever schooled
once your thoughts go past
her dress
   up on the wall with you
and us, we howling fool dogs
with draining cry eyes and fur tangles
and that old dog wheeze
sing the tune
trash can lit with fire
smoke from the manhole cover
every cliché
fingerless accidental gloves
brown oversized coat
driven to madness
from a good home
come join u on the wall
when your number
is not the one to call
   you turned like meat goes bad
like saturday seafood like eggs
like milk in the box in the fridge
next to the salt from the bag
of take-in

come on,
come in,
come up
   at 26,
she is fit to eat the lion
from his cage
and beat the eagle
to the sea
in a straight dive
yanked prey from his mouth
and the beak CLACKED
just air
come up here,
your eyes have burned from your skull
her gaze is upon your deep
and your soul
is next
you are the mall
no janitor can fix
join us on the wall
and sing the old songs
light the lanterns
a new prisoner
comes
ringing the break bell

Old People Are Raised/Make Room

come out from under the rocks,
you children
you basset hounds with new faces
you snarling gangs
cruel youth in small frames
sharing information
come out from under the rocks,
into the kitchen
in the door well
on the light spot
from that sun
going down on that street old people are raised
    gather in the swallowed hole
    where the grates come off
    the floor—for the third time
    it's all yours
come out to play with your copied keys,
you fearless mist
you spectator analyst
bad from the day you were born
and lipsticked
and lunged with words
muttered in the halls
of schools long past fitted for a damp drip
and an elbowed grunt
with slippers
and a senile bad back to fit
come in,
into the kitchen
in the door's place
under the bright rind
of orange day fade
burning down on that street old people are raised
and break our hearts
one by one
so we can die
a helpless death
and make room for the running of the word

Blueberry Sweat

this static in my mind
it reminds me of blueberry
sweat too
from fucking
and how flowers smell
when they accidentally come through an open window
not by the bed
but by the chair by the window
far enough from the bed
to make the light
be a bell
and bell-shaped
and fall into the curves of the pale skin and the sheets
plus that humming sound
not like an air conditioner unit
the big ones behind the buildings
those food emporiums now mostly abandoned
but that low hum
that says the day will be sweet
and i will receive a letter
or a postcard
with simple instructions
on how best i am loved
in the day
for my day's work
i miss the simple threads to my next encounter
and her heartbeat slow and steady
pure as snow
fucking beaten to bruises inside though from all her thinking
i miss that
that static in my mind
is the summertime sweet
or is it like the swing
teetering back and forth
pulling on the chain?
is the house full of dolls
or is it motherings
pink smoke
and a book of spells?
we can work it we can work it out
we can work it out
the work

is
to love
too much
and
blueberry sweat.

oh my we stole the show

we stole the show
she and i did dear
my goodness
did we ever
in the night's black cold
coal eyes
and snake constellations
etc. above her/us
we stole the show
and i stole her
she did not belong to me
though
bang clatter
something breaking in the kitchen
yelling screaming
fighting
exciting
in taxis in airplanes
always in hand
we settled in
we settled in
Lord
she stole my heart
for reals
and could rap alongside Nas
anyone
stunning
in perfect Oxford Queen's English
madness
madness
we stole the show
and the ending had to be as big as that
that beginning
love at first sight
true love
i never knew that before.
how long?
does a heart last after that
once the show is gone?
i am clinging to the seat
like it will play back
the kind of thing

you watch and watch again
or so shocked
you never can speak of anything again
oh my

Flickering

with my eyes
in the skull
back like
they were
flickering
muscles
tighter
than wires
i surrender
to the bed
and
let it have
at me eat
my today
feast on
my bones
gnaw on
my pores
this nap
or
revelations
or
succumbing
to
slippery
moments
either way
it is
something
else
entirely
and all
yes yes
yes yes
then
silence
with my eyes
in the skull
like a
deeper
drink
like

a dropped sink
on
a bounced
check of a day
cleared
by the banks
for
the fuck of it
yes yes
yes yes
slippery
then
silence
after the
clearing
is the
sheets up
and
limbs
out
and
hair a messed
wreck
of a
dreamed
desert sip
lips curled
around
the
drink
soda fountain
pink
and
very
fucking
yes
yes
yes
yes
and
release
with my eyes
in the skull
back like
they were
flickering

Wow, I'm Insane

Have you ever known a grief
so strange
it broke you into pieces of flames
and
hard-boiled eggs
insane
roaming table to table
in a lurch
with a hump
weighed soundly on your back
too many thoughts
to carry that weight?
have you?
dip-shits
fuck-face . . .
huh?
Have you seen that sign
with bulbs flashing in dust
the airborn soot
trampled under foot
and just gone
like a Sally Field haircut?
Well, it is by design
sometimes
to attract those asses into seats
to watch
me with all that me on fire and burning
as you went
as you left.
Have you ever known your grief by name?
huh?
Oh I have now, child, I have a degree
several degrees in burning
by your hands
when you weren't looking
with us not touching
my bones alight
each and every time
your name descends from a heaven
too far up
falling so fast
till it drills a hole through my bed

my bed a body
where no summertime is
for kicks
for whatever
wow
I'm insane
but just for now
for a kick
when I stutter
for lost things
gone sailing on brutal winds
on Christopher Cross yacht
hidden under my winter clothes
waiting to be discovered
there are no secrets
waiting to be discovered
I'm just insane
wow,
I'm growing old
I'm growing out
wearing thin
wearing out and rusting
just me, alonesque
living with Hope
that bitch
what am I, 9?
9 again
I was such a stubborn kid
allergic to the knowing
a love
it came and went
silently
without an end
and yet
this springtime scare
it is inevitable
and
something outside
inside the gray
it is growing
wow,
I'm insane.

Low Gong Goes the Clouds

Bells bells bells i hear bells
i turn off her lamp
i turn on her lamp
still not enough light
she is not coming back
i did this to myself
i call i write
she says all i want to do is fight
i am alone now

one day when the storms pass
this yard will be bare
bare of the trees and grass
and nothing will grow
i am covered
in snow
frozen
but you know
you know this about me
i turn on her lamp
i turn off her lamp
and i hear
bells
bells bells
the bells of doom
and i did this
to me
myself
wow

i hear for now
the inevitable
sound of bells
because bells sounds
right
thatsoundslikepoetrytome
anyways
i hear it for now
the glory and the line
clipped with my torso
when i come dashing by
in my yellow shorts

and sweatband
wait
NO NO NO NO NO
i do not see any of that
not mixed with bells anyway
what did it mean to ask myself
that just then
if i was good for
you know
another "win"
hell
i don't know
and i would not even if I did
even if I did
i would not know where to begin
about
all that glory
and
what someone might do with that
is this what a rumble with a loose goose
after a night on the town is suppose to be
for most you know without all that losing
on their mind
not on their mind
you know what i mean
is it
because
i am quite certain that must be a freedom like they had
before people were expected to know things about themselves
that kept them away from others in the night or day
in any way
once they felt like a beehive or a readied study
of a stinger's dozen
with more in the flock
just not in your hair
or under your shirt
No
i see buildings
rising with windows and offices
so much office-supply stuff in them
and
clicking and typing and i imagine people
people in sharp shirts and ties actually actually
typing
and

on the line with somebody
releasing the hounds
the dogs
heated only for a second and those numbers flying
and
perfect shapes of lost causes darting ceaslessly up the avenue
and shoppers shopping and people watching
from the tops of red buses not on the night loop
and fussing
with car horns and the rustling of bags everywhere bags
my god bags bags everything in them all around you
even when the street ends
and becomes the correct address
or the park begins or ends
this is our mess
and i
i hear for now the sound of bells
like
biblical and oughtta be horns
or trumpets with figurative angels
sitting there
blowing like hell
lunch mouthed and was it fish
or was it like a soup with fish
because the sound
is not the only thing
that
coming from your mouth
is so very very loud ha ha
i made a joke with figurative angels
involved
oh well
low gong
goes the clouds

pa-paw special

the truth is
i am always
getting my
feelings hurt
because they
are bigger
than me or
my hands
and i have
my grandfather's
hands
capable and daring
digits
ten
far from
zero
making
somethings
out of nothings
being a believer
these were things
he liked
and pranks
he loved them
i miss him every day
i miss his laughter
and his football commentary
and eating t.v. tray dinners
with him
and his war stories
and how
he loved my grandmother so
so
so much
he had a hat
he had a cane
he had an overcoat
and a suit for when
needed
and he fought in two wars
and cried
cried sometimes

silently
as i sat beside him
both of us looking
out into the light
shifting through
the spaces in the
leaves of the
magnolia tree
in front of the
house
where i really
grew up
he couldn't stand
Dave Letterman though
the way i can't stand
Carson Daly
so there was that
but
easily forgivable
for the man who
said to me once,
"Ryan, you are not like other children
you are special and it will be tough
but just never forget this
if you never forget anything in your life . . .
Never . . .
Bet . . .
Against . . .
Yourself."
my grandfather
That is who i would like to be
when i never grow up
for growing in.

Anxiety and Hope

Our City
It's a Jewel
Misted
and Hushed
By Its Own Hand
It Is a Fiction
And a Kid
Bubbled Up and Popped
Like a Thought
All Loud
and
Forgot
Like a Girl
Heels Dress and Gown
At a Ball
After the Ball Comes Down
And All Acquaintance
Be Forgot
Etc
Is Nothing
Compared to the Glass
When the Glass Got Dropped
on the Crystal Tile
Like That
In a Moment
So Fast
It Passes on the Street
In a Heat Flash
In the Flurries
of Holiday Bodies
and Cheer
Misted
and Hushed
Like my Old Heart
It's a Jewel
Our City
But without you
it's just glass and steel
reflection-pretty
and lonely
with a me inside it
feeling shitty

with hope
or
anxiety

Return to Santa

"hope,
did you have the party?
did you?
under the soft light of their fathers' money
and the
swift movement of capable arms of an electrician
specialized in illuminating rooms
for the lacking of heart
did you?
because i saw the red light on
way up in the terraced balconies
one looked almost fell
and i thought of you
and your friend
my loss
i never caught their names
their drunken clothes too expensive to name
as they rum-tongued each other
street-side
in the almost rain
you stood beside me
and didn't see
me
as i watched you mouth the lines of each amnesia kiss
was it her you wanted
or maybe
him—
to get to her;
you never know, with an allergic bundle of bad skin
they
grab your arm just right
and wrap those fingers tight
and that's enough
you know
to get me through a night
and like a fool
i dove right in.
hope,
did you bury the rest
did you make them stalkers too
even though
you have been separated by every one

continental
in hospital
or
worse, you imagined them—
a broken stone
at
each grave
you
dug with your bloodied fingernails
you bite
while you think you sleep soundly
in your perfect snore
in the dark
between lines of rude yellow light
you stole their favorite shirts too
i bet
that future-boys
they would have meaning too
did you
I didn't get enough dirt
you didn't dig deep enough
or did you think,
'oh, he is just a hick from the street
and his connections will do
those hicks, they grow tired
and
eventually sleep
so you can steal their shoes
and feel
what it is like
to be
a contender
in the ring
my face beaten into piles of bruises
and toothless smiling'
i can hear you
in the hall
it was foreign
but i understood it all
'oh daddy'
you will always be the one for me
fill it up
for another drink up in the country
with the man
who sold his project kid

for a box
for people to stuff their faces
full of slutpowders in
i should have split the sails
that night
alone
on one of those ships
in the piers of copenhagen
with my veins
and
lashed it into stuffing for future pillows
for your
useless night banging
and
perfectly acceptable excuses
later
when explaining
oh, hope
you know
she always has these things
we gather, no regrets
life is a fucking party
and we summon the spirits
of the coldest things
once
to be heard
twice
to be sold
you are so far from feeling
and
being a cutter
is just not anything but work
once
it ruins a loaner
you ice your soul down
with
elderly fat drunken thanksgiving turkeys
who have a job
destroying others people's life work
for more money
they would never use
attention is attention
and
that thing
you carry

like it was born into your hand
will turn
you back from stone
to flesh
one day again
if the galaxy is set free to balance itself
after your pummeling
of the naïve
if only a sign
from that other soulless fuck-face
god,
if only he was the perfect man
then
the rest of us
could all go home
back
to Santa
and
wait until
someone dreamed of being loved too much
elsewhere
on a planet
where
somehow
they forgot to make cowards
return to sender
address
North Pole
i was
a living present
for
some
asshole
and
god help,
i am sorry
but
today i don't feel so good
and
i don't care anymore
who loses
because
we
all know
when a man is left to his own ruined soul

it is never a matter of if
but
when"

For Your Tears

those people out there, who are they
intruders
bylines
and ghosts
fit to wreck it all in a night
take down the house
board by board
replace the walls with bottles
emptied out one by one
till we are see-through
like souls at sail
souls at sail
on fire
water in the pails
allergic
and getting higher
   draw me a map of those stars
   and i'll sleep in here
and you will die a little
for your tears

Orange

A hand to touch
   A fit, to mask or shake just what
   It is January or not
Time splinters off in a drool well
It rains or it stops raining
A sink clogs or it stops draining
The mask falls off
   A new bouquet swells
   A sneeze lets loose
In the house the animals stir
The print on the couch dwells
It lets go of its color
And the light fades
   What color is that?
   What moment is that?
   What figure is drawn?
   On what eyes?
   A child yawns
   A seat on the bus is closed
This light, This year, This hour
It multiplies itself by the word
It goes soup on the bowl
And the bowl draws near
Its color revealed
   A kind sleep
   A hellish dream
   On my skin that sun goes orange
   And I burn myself
   And my eyes cave in
This horror of time clicks my heels
It laughs that laugh of cruel poses
Our dreams are not our collective
But submission is easier
When we pretend this together
   A fantasy a clock
   A hand designs hour not hands
   A minute exposes cracks
   A time forgets us
   A stop
   My eyes hurt
   It is too much
   Orange

We Paint Together

we paint together
something smallish
crooked wirey
dissolving like gray candy
on white dinner plates
and i talk and i talk
and i t a l k
i am so full of shit
and i don't know i don't know
till i hear us talk
when you talk like adults
and i am trapped
like a kid in a boxy room
my mouth shuts
a trapped door
and piles of dirt
for brooms
sweeping the ends of the earth
for rainbows
i feel like i misspell
when the thoughts come put
    out
like collected cows
flatulent and cross
like city weather
i am a subway map of the stars
trains do not go
to
yet.

Writing, Dying, for the Trying

in ten seconds
an alley cat
will rush through the marshes
and break the glass
into my arms
with a bucket full of cash
   and i will still be here
   sober sober sober
   writing dying for the trying to get right
in no quick succession
a gang of ducks
will surrender the enemy
haven just given up
like a train cliché
running through my head banging
   and i will still be here
   helplessly helplessly sober
   writing dying for the trying to get right
when the belly
laughs
when the head
hurts
when the bed
groans
when the mind
goes
i will still be sitting here, with you, or not, buried inside this, almost alive,
talking to no one
   writing dying for the trying to get right

The Statue of Liberty Is French, Asshole

Shock sets in
the blast of the hot air touches her face
like a lover might have
with hot electric sand mouth
and cabinets inside her
made of grot
from over the ocean
a witty french girl with spikes
almost mossy
a shade of green
sick tone
the statue of liberty
is on the outs tonight
for a hot bang
in the
stinking piles
of garbage in Brooklyn
Oh, you know
roof parties
and
and sensible girl gives it up
one night a week
i mean
one night a year
in that same
that
same dress
how
are
they to know that
those
easy boys all of them those easy boys
you
are
so
stupid
fuck you
says the Statue of Liberty
to Brooklyn
pissing
into
an

ocean of
dead
bodies

I Am One of Those

I am one of those
Satisfaction machines
coal dust sooting the hillsides with ash
and sky gone gray night after night
day after day
always
long machine moans and out of context it's beautiful
to a fool
then comes the Scotch
and the cigarette stains
and the food floor and the blanket gets sauced
with burn marks
and pocketed shirts for cigarettes
bad-breath dreams
and no dog because the dog stays with the girl
and girls don't like their alcoholics when the dust settles
and they dream of their father dying
and no amount of night is enough
for an unsettled stomach
in a girl
so pushing past the dresser drawer to be pilfered through
looking for notes from a boy not me
and socks and things i don't understand
comes the bitter parts of panic
and outside the stars sing into plastic cups
into trucks of cars and beds of trucks
tailgated in the suburbs
New Jersey parking lots filled up with yesterday's puddles
reflecting the lights of some steel plant
consumed with people roaches and rats
and Disney dreams
and me
and my bad habits
screaming commands to their children my years of pain
my past
and I fuck them over for every day straight
wrenches in the Satisfaction machine
and a great white fuck you
to everything I was
But inside
I am still one of those

The Whole Universe Is God's Shithole Apartment Complex

this whole thing is an organism
a machine
i count endless stars
like atoms and space between them
we're bugs
bugs on the cell
bringing down the house
and the house is fell
this whole universe is a trap
with hair
i bet probably or not
something with some kind of eyes
these flickering stars
its tiny insides
i still want to fuck her on the hillside
though
i am just that way
built out of dreams
and particles
a particle machine spitting clouds
and ash
cussing up flags and money slots
bickering
shitty and mad
swollen and green
from not using myself like i ought to
or being clean
i am though
just something
like a tiny thing
inside the breathing monster
i am a part of the insides
made out of oceans
like one of its dreams

Infinity Blues

chapter III

I REFUSE

I refuse to edit*
I am but a single life
I refuse to edit
look away
if you choose
but these bulbs
will burn in cycles
if forever
was a single night

*Editor's Note: This poem was originally 32 pages long. —JT

Alit Daffodil

oh,
wasn't your lover from here, alit daffodil?
hmmm
i eat his food
they serve me and smile
i compliment the chef
for i cannot help myself
not born
into the coin
myself
i was born into a love of things
with the lights on
gunfire came later
mashed potato
when i say a thing is good
a mouth
someone's
it just opens up
and the teeth come out as the lips resurface
without the knowing
for the lighting of the grin
of a truth
blinding its way in,
doll-face
—you call it charm
—i call that being warm
and i agree to disagree
still
you are a plastic
invisible menace
and mean
as snakes
mean as snakes pissed on
on fire
oh,
and HIM
"a writer" you say with a smirk and a grin
that tells me where he's been
he worked, what?
8 hours a day
and saved himself for you
for two years

and he's FRENCH . . .
ha ha ha
that's funny
i bet he did
S U R E
because
you loved loved loved his lashings
and like a shark
you were helpless in his arms
because you must never stop moving
and once the blur of gray
went into fins
and madness
you could both reach full potential
as losers together
causing mutual sadness
upper-class voodoo
what money does to bright children
with bad names
plucked up from novels
two shelves up
up a fucking ladder
bathing in the glow of a room of air
poor people would breathe in
hungry
with hungry stares
if only they could eat you
in the alpines
where all was fair
so
I buy a book then
(of course not his—
he couldn't publish
if his mother sold the house
and bought xerox
held his hand in front of a pillar of blank white paper
and begged
words do not come from eggs
asshole)
nobody coughing over their shoulder
making a sound like a cough
if it went HA CC KKKK
spoiled first he was self-served
THEN became a brat
(one must allow ample time at university for that)

oh, and plenty of hip-hop
white people on porches memorizing rap
about setting themselves free
from your fucking parents' money trap
and corporations companies
and
however many fucking people
they could summon with fire truck hoses and baseball bats
i wish they could punch your ancestors
in the face
for every noose
because you created a class system
when you were born
your parents' lawyers advising them
if you want to pretend to be human
you'll need evidence
(somebody grab the aftermints)
him
get a typewriter before his fingers go flat
and his mother's suit's damp
not wet
it's the upper east side, for god's sake
and they have words for that
for what i am
and then
and after the wedding
which "just came up"
with entire villas reserved
plus
master-planning
my payment of your airline ticket
notwithstanding
don't forget
to bring the photos of the orgy
and reminisce
it will be good for the book,
he says
that one he never writes
for writing
is written
so
so i buy the bad ones close enough
in the clearance bin
one for every hundred push pins
i find words he would use

and i stick them in
i imagine his eyes
and
what adorns that face
and dream a swarm of hornets
hovering with pulsing stems
of unicorns unstoppable
with fangs
trampling his bones
crushing his limbs
and pirates
named Jephry
dressed as businessmen idle and unbusy
with friends with names like Hank and Lou
marrying your daughters
your mouth's agape
as they off them to the suburbs
where
track housing and television dreams
eventually bury them
except their souls
which they suffer through their children
your legacy
your second generation
for
every wasted word
i demand a shift
when i light the candle
i make a wish
black
black as a fucking hole
in the universe
in the walls
of the house of the damned
and i smile
perfect timing
perfect pitch
on note over coffee
not even trying
half smoking a cigarette
and
i saturate this place with my scent
like a tiger let loose
on the wronged
and i am screaming mad and covered in sweat

devouring every moment
you lied
like i was starving and blind
for love
which i was
thumbing the wall for anything
anything that felt alive
or like a switch
i needed a light
you gave me a church burning
with eyes of amethyst
but get this,
get this,
when the bottom comes up, if this ship is intact
on its side
you will salute a ruin maybe
a revenge, not likely
done unto a thing
because
i am alone
in my lost
and
in this fire
we do not burn together
us,
separated only by the lines
of mistrust
waiting on the roller-coaster rides
in that endless ring
of unneeded desires
broken
for how hard you hit it
the last time it rang
now it's rung
a rich person's problem
up comes another museum
because
i was just a fantasy fuck
a cinemax
and i will always be better
and so much more
than that
your mother's daughter, you certainly are not
but also
they will know that

for genius always "outs"
and if nothing else
coin-born book of skin
any old whore can be something great
but to be a knower of a home
and refuse
to be better banged
with a later coming eventually and steady
down the midnight shift of the telephone
that was mine
is surely just another slut with wheels
waiting for another to be trapped
and caught under your horrid tasteless heels
those get-away sticks
with trashy give-aways
stuck on the bottom
matching
in tweed and twit
so
from his home country
in my labored rest
i say fuck you
assholes
you deserve it all
and
all the best
i hope you are happy
and ready
for the balance is so strong
and steady
even it penetrates through
the houses of the printers
of the slavery you call money
honeybee
so thanks
it's like i got out of jail for free
with a silent
golden pardon
now if you will excuse me,
back to my book
my perfect omelette

Baltic Sea

Baltic Sea
that was her
at night with the striped socks, legs exposed
under the quilt
watching t.v.

Baltic Sea,
whatever, ok, whatever
she would say
over and over
over and over
eating ice cream
straight from the container
uninterested in conspiracy
or
laughter
or
fucking
even

i can remember pictures though
fucking some man in a villa
at a goddamn wedding
much like the one you know
she was attending
while i walked the coast-lit lined beaches
of Amsterdam
furious
bloodletting
into myself
Baltic Sea

so confused of the night
i am a tugboat
hauling with me terrors and sight
empty of horizons
the sway only of the waves
and the endless crossings
of oceans
in efforts to elaborate my plays

so where were you that night

if not in that picture
with that man
Baltic Sea
heart like a fire engine on fire
in the snow
awful lover stuttering bedroom talker
and slow
huh Baltic Sea
"i don't know anymore," she says, "i dunno."

ha ha ha

for a nickel
and a laugh
we
we got touched by a ghost
in the ghost house
ha ha ha

it cost
like, a nickel
but you pay later
because
well, you know why cause

after you walk out the back
and that place
it looks like the back of any place
the back parking lot like
you know,
where the Real ghosts are
well
you know you done it now
and
ain't no use pretending now
just get in
get in the car
    and when
when she drives you home
you go in
and now,
now this is your world
not hers
that is haunted
and you
you
that's fucked
for a night of peace

for a nickel and a laugh

ha ha ha

i can see you still

oh my mouth won't say your name
it says (   )
like treasures
in a chest
so many
a sea could digest
and i
i am the drag of the pulley
at the end of the sea
and the pier
tied with shift-ships
sailing into port
i am still
i see those birds
those seagulls
pesty critters
picking at the popcorn
while you and i
you and i, we ride the rides
at that place
where the subway ends
or used to
on that line
lines after avenue
X, Y, Z, and Q
i think of you now
as i imagine all of it is
your face, so many
stars
i feel the ships pulling in fast
and then slow,
you know
too aware of a dock
to collide
and make them feel the water inside
new eyes
like when you and i were young
younger
and from the well
we drank each drop
like it grew up
each bone

you kicked your leg against the gravel
outside the restaurant
me
across the street on the telephone
now i sleep all bad
and dream of being at sea
at one with an ocean
like so many treasures
like
how i think of you as i write this
your face,
so many
stars

At a Distance

At a distance it moves
this thing in me
that growls at my gut
it plays strange games
with cards
and sneers at me
from the shadows
it stays SUPER busy
when i escape
i am lucky
if only for an instant

At a distance I can see myself
a grown man aged 33
but none at all in years
if those years mean
each one
like a fallen wall not a built thing
a piece of mortar maybe
missing from the bright
morning-side wonder
thrown through a window
by a child
because
becausewhy
maybe then, yes i can see myself
but at a distance

at a distance from myself
from you
from everyone
safe enough
that you might never get through
i know that i do not know
and that neither do you
not your gods
nor your books
not your analyst
not your family of crooks
because
like all things
they too

they too will pass us by, as we pass
and fade into the dry-mouth
of history
barely a stain
on a rug of electricity
floating in space
so,
pardon me if i grow up already
i see
something shiny
beautiful maybe
over that way again
at a distance
but my feet will never give
not even if they were but a bone
stuck bone through
a tennis shoe
i was there
i was standing in front of you
my hands were out
i held a heart the size of a question
up to you
with marvelous affection
star-struck from heaven
like an ocean made of everything
a love has ever given
but
not too close
at a distance
i felt the spit
and that
that is that
i guess.

Babydoll

let's just take three hands
one free
and make a machine
that sweats
on summertime beds
pour a glass
of sweet tea
over our heads
ok,
or
instead,
let's build bridges from here to Leningrad
with lights attached
that fade
into the hyper-lit orange sun parade
because
we
us folks
don't talk about our feelings
no
not us
of course, unless it is too late
and
the night is at the door
rapping away
on the metal handle
wood shaking
our endless ceilings
babydoll
i
i am not your feelings.

A New Party of One

goddamn heavy strings of shiny purple
shoelaces
with cherry print
tied
in a bow
go
on top of a box
with pages
—this thing i make from words
to be given
at once, suddenly
to her
and be forgot
        or
swallowed and drowned
with sugar on top
        also
from a spoon
is the nectar in my lungs
suffocated like a scream
round my tooth
for the only girl i knew
        who
makes me go lost
like a shaking a curse
    or cops
if she or i were a punk
    with
eyes on the stranger
past a hot dog stand
body and soul all tired
    again
        or
white snow flurries come
onto cars
and the sides of buses
onto the christmas body rushes
she sees an old lover
but i have given her to me
        and i go
    a given thing
now as a gesture

of closure
for
this awful thing

a new party of one

did you see?

   did you see that?
fast fast fast
letters turning to ice
like winter breath
those nights
gosh they came and went came and went
i am not at the party
not dancing
not laughing
not drinking
not holding a glass
not seeing your dress
not under a moon
not with you
not facing east or west
did you see the witches moon
it hovered and stalled
like a car under piles of wet
puddles oil snakes dancing
inside them like metal rainbow worms
in that dirty mix
i am not with you inside that room
not under stairs
not under lights
not hearing music
not talking
not knowing if it's alright
you are not putting your hand on my knee
i am not breathing
i am not at that party
not tonight
i went
fast fast fast
did you see?
did you see?

i think i thought i loved you

i think i thought i loved you
i always did
vampire eyes
milk skin

i think i thought i loved you
how you moved, your body
ownership driven
natural slave runner

i hate you
your matching pairs
your split ends
your dying figure
   your shadow
i hate you
your collapsible will
your petty drip
of a wordless silence attempt
you bite your lip
moons crack

you looked like a hill
climbable
of clouded rose
tree spirit and blue-eyed explosions
of marble-headed jar break
on the cement
full-on spring
light everywhere blasting

but my how evil are you are you
tornado t o r n a d o
in a neighborhood
soft
with us quiet dreamers

i think i loved you
your power pains
your hungry stomach
your hair falling out
your scraping shower gloves

pink and blue
i think i thought i loved you
in the shower
trying to remove yourself
from your own body
into a drain

clogged
like my mouth forever silenced in awful
horrid
disgusting pain
i hate you
i hate you
my god
once
once in a while
i think i thought i loved you

Your Side Now

on your side now
is books
i moved the pillows
up top
like they forgot
or i did
but we did not
me and the pillows know
something's missing
and the room
the room does too
it sighs
when i come in
the door
when i arrive
thinks i am you
and sighs
or is that me
my insides
hmmmm
i scare myself
see my shadow or myself
in the mirror
sometimes both
i sigh too
on your side now
i leave the phone
the books and space
any single lifetime takes
if it took breaths
like it climbed
a summertime hill
all day
that bed
so sad
it limps and lies down
shuffleboard headed
old
and
on your side now.

enough rope

if only i had enough rope
i would lasso that moon
down
and deliver it to you
even though
it would split the ocean
and the sea
in twos
and threes
i would beg for your mercy
i would cry at your knees
god
i miss you so
you have no idea you know
i am lost
this place in time, where is this, what is this, why
why did we do this?
to me
it is done
by us both
the isolation
and speculation on, how much rope
is enough
enough rope
i am imaginary letters
hopeless telephone feathers
zero till fade
i am white-out
ghost after ghost
33 and in ruins
i am research now
a controlled experiment
for her favorites
i am in the out box
no return address and no topics
a landmark
a call for help
red
surrounded by three guides
truth beauty and justice
a t.v. screen
i once walked across—cowboy-boot drunk

on a glistening ship of a night
a four-post bed
where everything that happens
is only something in my head
in my mind
and outside
it might as always be snowing now
for the lack of going out
or in
how sad
how sad
and this
this is no way to begin
but i take meaurements
to keep me sane
to validate
what is real
and
what is pretend
just for now
just in case
how much
is enough
enough rope.

Closed

closed
that is what i am today
closed
robbed
isles fucking broken
baseball batted
winged
with colorful sweets scattered
all over the floor

God, I hit my knees that day
and wanted so bad
just wanted to say
"please, please bring her home,
back to me . . ."
but all my mouth
could sputter
with tear dribble
was,
"i am so weak"
"i am so weak"
like a record player
floating in space
forever on repeat
water
running down my snotted face
from my eyes
at the foot of the bed
head touching the throw blanket
i used to fuck her on
and sleep next to her in
Jesus,
what a thing to feel
the eyes of Brahman
and us
upon the wheel

and in that moment she was on a beach just then
with an old man who collects million-dollar checks
from taking people's businesses from them
and breaking them into things he can sell
their hearts ripped out first

and placed at the ferry well
eventual ice-box dinner food
microwaved
and fit for moveable trays
and football games coming
those poor people of the long winter
a fat fuck with a driver, a car
and some special foreign name
on a beach,
two of them,
him, at least 50-something
while I was asking God,
asking God for someone
God,
who must be so busy his doorbell is bloody
on a beach
the two of them
i saw a photograph later
and puked
into the toilet
my guts
for what I had left of love
or the knowing

closed
that is what I am now
closed
robbed
riddled with effects
of a clearance sale
when everything goes
but the walls
skin and bone
so lost
and
closed

Brass

. . . when
when the brass blows
down that crooked lane
is that when
is that when you will
you know
say my name
once more
and
maybe even cry
no
no i doubt that
very
very
much
. . . when

Terrible

in the days of a man's life once in a while
it happens,
where you see the whole thing
a whole life
on a carton of milk as plain as day
like you picked your own pockets
and your heart alights
and you see
all
the
way
down,
to the end,
in the days of a life,
as a man might,
i have peeked into that room
maybe once or twice
at the shining ember
the ash
of a life
that i once had and it keeps me
and it demands
demands
i steer this into worse waters
further i go
obeying its commands
a death's
each time
because inside tough guys inside men
is just nothing but
crocheted lined dangling legged walls
of afraid kids
making up names for things
telling ghost stories
while the walls rattle
of something cruel
something terrible
just
outside
the
door.

Carnations

missed birthday
forgotten
slipped my mind
under the door in the doorpile
of forgots
and a fistful of carnations
just browning on the edge
that was NOT me
not me
i had a silent view of the backside of the buildings
and i looked through
and i saw a family
a couple
their privacy
untouched by my sitting in the chair helpless
alone
wondering where were you
and where was i
and what does it mean
when the bedroom
says,
"maybe lie down now and don't get up"
and,
"i will hold you in a dream until you close"
clutching a cold cell phone
wondering
helplessly
dying to show more love
like an animal
feasting on the remains
of a carcass
of my own dried bones
in the desert
with two blankets at the foot of the bed
one blue
one brownish red

Goodnight Little One

when the ship goes funny
you know, on the sea
like the bed were a boat
is that you?
or is that me?
because i lost my glasses
like two summers ago
and i can't fucking see
for shit

i dream more about the desert now
which is better
less animals and sand traps
less chance of civilization
people like you
    and your friends
so shallow
when you die
you will look the same
like laughing rattling bones
on pirate ships
smiling like corpses
surrounded in gold
i fucking hate you

your shallow madness

anyway,
i am almost home
and my ship is flying steadily through the air
tonight i am going to go find something to send me
sixteen thousand times higher
than air
and look down on you
as i die
and laugh
as i return to the part of the sun i am of my father Ra
and wish doom upon the parts of you
that destroy yourself
your ability to heal
or anyone
and you will live again and again many times before you learn

i can hardly see for the
rays in my father's
cauldron

so goodnight little one

Every Time

every time
each tide
each continental drift
each and every time my house must move,
my apartment,
my whatever,
for all the loose things in it
i did not know
until today
one was you
that they could move
become displaced i knew
but you
or us
in that brown shadow of a wall
could go into the mellowing
if it grew darker
in time
and left us yellow
and like smoke
in the room spinning out
and upwards
and into the draft
and toward the places in the window
where bigger things were kept out
and people too kept out
some people
where smoke goes
hurling into the safety of a wind
outside
this vaccum
of home
something dies
every time

Real Fucking Dreams Come True

forget the sea that drug your body ashore
and the murder
if that is what you wish to imagine
this heartache was
because
like something in a dream
this did not happen to you
it happened with you
and
you don't care
you
really don't fucking care
the
champagne will be aboard a boat
the streets will be made of cobblestone
and
the moon will be yours
you will recover
but
when love takes the very thing from you
that made you what you were before
by fire must your bones alight
and
your soul should not return
for true love
is
more
more than the money's worth
and on good advices are the graces of the gods
the seas are parted
and
the waves are long
for
the hunters
when
the innocent scream and theirs are the words of pain
recognized
by
a fateful world
with
a merciful law
of

ebb and tide
and
for that
any shore is too expensive for a loss
when it could walk away and leave in dust
nothing anyway
and
keep those others talking distracted anything
but
in the way
of
those here to concern the world again
with laughter
and
real fucking dreams

Sit Down

when the house goes quiet
and she stops
you know
moving around inside me
i can see her
smiling
made of flesh and bone
heavy as a jewel factory
and bright inside
and brick outside
with lights
lights on
and the sound of typing
endless and still
moving through my head
on the windowsill
basking her in unneeded light
we made it through
summer
winter
not always night
but we made it through
to this
this end
when the bells crack
and the door gives
and all a man can do when he feels her go
who doesn't drink or die
is sit down for a second
and thank God
she was born
and cry

too much night

If I were as mean as I would like
I would be small
and
your stolen bike
I would
go
get it from thugs
and
beat some asses
but
we don't talk anymore
and
I will never hear you laugh again
because
we left
and
it's over
and
one of us had trouble letting go
so
no bike
and
just me
and
lots and lots and lots and lots
of
questions
and
too much night

infinity blues

nobody is going to be able to save me
and i AM going to die
but not old
and not slow
but suddenly
in a flash
i mean, a truck may go past
maybe i slip because i am tired
maybe i know to slip
but i can't watch beautiful women go by me anymore
and grow old
and lose my grip
and know my words are lessened by the days
the dark days of the artless
i am a fucking fool
you know
for thinking this is poetry
or that anyone would care at all
i don't address you
when you read
because it was only one girl i wanted to need
who i wanted to write to
or for
only one set of legs
for me to set the seed
i am a dirty old fuck on the inside
but not
i am all kinds of trinkets and Southern things
forget
spoiled by loneliness
and made of forgot
i am rot
and i AM going to die
and it won't matter because you all will be dead soon enough too
time does this
and i'd rather slip
into the tarmac
into the ocean
unnoticed
like i was
like it were
than feel this kind of pain and know i am only turning green

from new growth
i could never stand
i am not fit to be an older man
not now
nor ever again
i am broken like the lamp on the nightstand
i am the ghost on
the foot of the bed
i am
a pair
of her shoes
and obsessed
like i am supposed to be
and filled up full gut
with infinity blues

In the Middle of the Night Goes the Bang

in these slow moments, when there is too much time, i feel the entire inside
world of me collapse into its pile
the words drift from me
and i am but a calm swarm
an endless end
my skin touches the edge of the desk and i know i am alive
sort of hanging
and i feel a soft heart
my own
go into the gears, go shredding
for lack of tears
and more words
for the things i could not express
and time
which will not wind itself back
where the folds of what was me and what were wishes
came undone
like a slow dress in a brutal wind
like when a flock separates
and takes no shape again
was that my soul
my heart wrapped in tin
with a wire
on ice
and a bulb too thin
or a dream too long
or a breath too kissed
words they do fine
but cannot touch
this thing i miss
a heart
inside me
when
in the middle of the night goes the bang

Lighthouse

when a woman leaves
she leaves
and leaves
with scents
and all the smells
of the house
when a house is calm
go
with
her
she takes with her the essence
of a place
painting the insides invisibly
while you were not looking
or shall i say, i

when a woman leaves
her smells
are small
hells
each much nastier than a sting
burned into your bed
in a fiery ring

and with her went the candles too
white ones, delightful ones
lit from time to time
shining
when she left she took the pictures
too
no diety confusion
or something
either way my retinas are masked with shadows of lines of the burn mark of her
face inside
tonight i missed
that scent
that smell
which is why i sleep with her sweater
it is still there
fading in the rest of a wooden ship
with a white flag
and battered sail

from storms passed
where calm is now
a lighthouse is a lighthouse with or without
a light

The Rushes

The house shook with horrible thunder
so we went inside
where the noise was
coming from

The spaces in
between the words
became a line
so we went under
the house
then over the spaces
with words

The words were not
enough
to keep her in my
dream
i am almost about
to speak
and
i awake

the house shakes
like
my hands shake
not
someone else's
but
by themselves

The house and i
shake and
everything else
is moving
not me or us
it is a none-of-my-
business earthquake
this day
and
you know,
i have seen these
colors once but they

blurred by the
rushes of
disappearing

i'm a sick man, buttercup

a sick man sits curbside, morningtime
papers just being lifted from
oversized doors
leading into the catacombs of homes
and thinks,
"when i am old, or not, and pass
i hope i become
a cloaked witch in the woods
behind your regal house
and my eyes are hollow
and eaten out by birds
and your children will see
my shadow
in the hall
and in the woods
i will haunt them
and they
will know the name of the abandoned"
then launches back upon the bench
and thinks of a laugh
and skin
softer than a cotton patch
in a cloth basket
and breasts like imaginary tears painted blue on a canvas 9 feet tall
and calm
and as the wind kicks up
a bag
and throws it round
the square he thinks,
"but i will be tired by then
and my soul
so tired now
is like the kind of cry
that becomes so inaudible
it is not a mumble
but like the constant
clicking of a greyhound
throwing a rod
quietly, trying to cut off
its gasoline supply

and i have become

the actions
of a man
ready to light himself
with something stronger than fire
to erase even
these last moments of
total
fucking
regret
and
despair"
and then has eggs
takes medication
for posttraumatic
events
and
collapses
on a bed
of fine silk
where
he never belonged
because
i
will
never
fucking
belong
to
anyone
again
despite my mumbling senile heart
rocked into its useless place
by
every
unknown
betrayal
and
line
that could have taken lovers anywhere
but
left one
to
question
why a man is even born
with pure

desire
and
hope
hope is as dead as the pigeon
floating
in the water
below the statue
in the tank
those new showers
will
wash his wings
into the gutter
where
i
am,
buttercup

I Fucking Miss You

To not be with you.
my God
my world just ends
goes calm
before me in a darkness
like a night
is a darkness
i strike
inside me
that moment
and
all i see
our hands
together
enclosed
around a light
it was simple gestures
not fuss
that kept me in the deep
protected by us
if I could
I would build those walls
back up
but they went Jericho
from backwards wishing
rung as clouded bells
for the missing
of your touch
upon my life
as i sit here so far from a home
written in your chest
i am sorry
for every moment now
i wasted
taking breaths
thinking
i might have that chance
to hear that soft laughter
forever
a jewel into the oceans
a bread crumb trail
ends

and i don't know
i am so sorry
so sorry
i fucking miss you.

Hammer It Home, Slugger

Last night
i had that stupid dream
again
where i am in jail
so horrible
i should wake up relieved
but i am not
me
depressed in a puddle of pillows
and lint
a newspaper
unfit to print
or a dull sauce
dream-lost
and
it wouldn't be so bad
if i didn't know inside the place
that it would never be loneliness
that waited for me
to break my face
but me alone
separated in a cosmos
where i couldn't stroke her neck
of hair
outside somewhere
she is cornered, scared
with me locked tight
with me not there
but it is just selfish
of me
you know
that i would care
to defend
a woman against her own dreams
from my head
to my knees
you shouldn't have,
really,
lying like you should
in a loved bed
why don't you
you know,

hammer it home, slugger
and call it
before
it's too late
and
neither of us will win.

That Door Is Closed

fixed red sign; too bright;
blasting neon
red brick cloaked
in darkness
and
noise
two bodies pass the gated store
this is a nighttime fantasy
you say
"you say" that
THAT
to yourself
with panic, a body fidget
and
it's like
somebody was not there
and
closed the doors
Dear me,
That Door Is Closed
That Door Is Closed
but
like a new thing in a new cage
i find the wall
with my face
and
etch the wall
for the future remembered dark fixture fingering
but
this is not that house
nor a home
i knew
past present or drawn by hand
in blue and white
this
is
a
fantasy
now
but worse maybe
but worse maybe
but worse maybe

but worse maybe
see what i am doing
i am writing it out
i am writing it out
i am writing it out
i am
i will
i was
i know
THAT DOOR IS CLOSED
THAT DOOR IS CLOSED . . .
but, but////// . . . .
but . . . .
but fuck.
fuck.
fuck fuck fuck fuck
fuck
that is what.

Cocooned

i break the seal on the sea
i enter the water
all done by noon
in a bath
or by shower
and off off off i go
into my milky broadway
into my world
i count the rings on the tile
i clean awhile
it's never too soon
in a minute
goes the hour
and off off off i go
into my wordless tower
into my static
rainbows with new colors
seeds with seedpodflowers
motionless whirligigs
and godknowswhat
really
banging around in the cracks
i do not say her name
it would break my back
and splinter my shield
and i am just made of small dreams
and tough talk
and fight
and a weakness for privilege and might
we lost it
i lost it
so
i break the seal on the sea
i enter the water
but i do not leave
every wave in the ocean now stays
wrapped in her name
cocooned

Where?

where
where could i go?
like this.
swollen from head to toe.
salty as a tear
inside a sea
bothered like a sail
on a worn beach
workmen's prints
up each side
scattered
for the love of god.
where
where could i go?
if i were a dream
i would meet us
like a mitten
gray cloud
over us snowing
in our hair
in the city
your hand in mine
my fingers
on yours
locked
i loved you so much inside me
i swallowed it up
me in a cup
my skin
stars
in the air outside and between
in a single word
in a thought
of you
where
where could i go
now?

My Favorite . . . Ever

you were my favorite
and i pushed you away
so foolish
so so so
foolish
and then wrecked myself against the rocks
like a doll
to the floor
with myself
then you
and it broke
b r o k e
you
with reason
and beauty
and grace
loving me
so reckless
we were
reckless
i was
and now
this moment
this body
feels trapped
in sickness
in grief
like
i slipped out of time
into a thing
a place
that should not be
and
i cannot break the spell
of this moment
ever

I Make Myself Sick

I make myself sick
Really
Fawning over a lampside table turning blue and red
and blond, all of a sudden
sitting in the middle of the room
surrounded by particle accelerators
and trash
Like I could drink the whole of the ocean
and browse through the fish
that lie at the bottom of what was the ocean
to find one perfect for my dish
I make myself sick
Really I do
I'd rather ring you up and leave you be
to be alone
than meet you there
and have to disclose what it is I do not have
sick
generator noises armpit stinks
dry heat and basement sweat
and blue eyes
this is the lot of the crime
I'm parking cars here all the time
dreamless ass-face
discovering nothing
taking as much to disappear as needed
in phrases until mutter comes
or dawn
or both
and I trash my inside to reflect walls with receipts
and directions to nobody's house covering it.
sick sick sick
and nobody calls.
I got a blue idea
a blue idea for a blonde
and neat rows of teeth gone crooked from crime
and bum notes
and cash
I wanna try to remember what it was that made me happen so fast
or kill it in one go
paint a target on the ceiling of my room
and open my eyes one morning

surrounded by somebody better than me
and prettier than you
sick sick sick sick
I make myself sick
and this is why you love me.

Red

Red
sleeping in the pile
of pillows
blueberry gardens
in her closed
freckled eyes
lids shut soft
under a halo
of curls and fire
Red
dictionary legged
brittle
closes the book
and returns to the rock
with her light
ships gone mad
she signals
into the frenzy of white
water
Red
    do you hear my voice inside your head
    when you see a pitiful thing?
    do you like to watch the weak ones fall
    when you see a weakness giving?
Red Red Red Red Red
go on, put your hand in his hand again
dance with someone
everything is music and lights
shining in the ballroom dresses
and shoes and feather caps
silver and gold and gray
clouds
out the window where we are
where i am in the hustling
crowds of winter coats and bodies
slightly drifting further down
the river of tar
and broadway in calm
swift movements of panic and loss
my life
was
Red

sleeping in the pile
of pillows
blueberry gardens
in her closed
freckled eyes
lids shut soft
under a halo
of curls and fire

soon it will be time to go

soon it will be time to go
the kids will lead
the adults
to the jackets and coats
by the door
and rattling upon the floor
near the shoes
will be the encore
for the night
and once the handle turns
the first ones go
the dark street outside
will suck us all dry
from our skin
to our bones
into it
and we will scatter like seeds
on a single flower
single
rainflowers
and in that house
the music will dim
the table a mess
a wreck
only plates
of bones
and i will know the names
and faces
burned into my eyes
like
a book with no spine
and endless pages
because if not now
soon

Spit Hits My Face

once she spits in your face
not really
but close
close like everything done is fuck you
close as a person gets
before their spit flies from their mouth
and lands on your cheek
warm and smelling of salt
and filth
it is over
but a war
that i won't win or fight begins and all inside a head
      to kill the one who went inside them
that is the fucking curse
is having this dick
and this ability with words
and meaning shit
that is the fucking reason everything is fuck you and spit hits your face without
a sound
      and her not even there
      who is fucking
      who is sleeping from depression
      who cares
fuck fuck fuck
a bottle of seltzer
some cotton swabs
a cutting razor
band-aids
a piece of flesh-colored tape
cut
cut
cut
till it feels like it did when you would make yourself sick
and vomit
in case you weren't perfect enough
in case we went too deep and someone said i love you
spit hits my face.
every night
here
alone
guilty as a dogbone
chewed up

off the roof of a speeding car
thrown
beheaded by truth
dethroned
from my tower of bullshit
thank you
no
seriously
spit
spit
spit
spit hits my face
forever
forever
i deserve it.

It's Time

it is time for me
to turn
the rope round the dolly
and cast the boat
back
into the sea of black
concrete and tar
and take the things i believe
are me
with me
away from the grilled cake
of this apartment
and i am just numb
and sad
and rooftops bruised
with sun and snow tan
and madness
minus the act
somewhere in the past
i turn your face into a laugh
all the way from your stomach
and we lie quietly
and sleep
cheek to cheek
like children
who found each other in the woods
hungry
and in need of sleep
and
if i stay inside that dream
one more week
i will die here
an old woman
for the loss of you
in my old man clothes
growing old with you in my dreams
like an electric blueberry tree
on pills
sweet and not mean
and
i'd rather go out there and fight
fight for it

till i run out of steam
i'd rather fish
now
but won't because they all know
i'd throw them back
who could eat
in times like this
but you, or people starving hungry
so i untie the rope
and push myself back
and off i go
off
into some new unknown
sad
like you never seen

I Am a Cemetery

so i am a cemetery of new ideas again today
yay
i got greased by lightning and terrified
and whatnot
went to the diner
and it felt bad bad bad
i walk steadily alone
by myself
with the new one
and even today she said,
"it feels like there is a ghost in the room"
so there it is
again
you
so i am a cemetery of new ideas again today
patches of clouds of red hair
faint laughter
i resume doing nothing constantly
i am becoming like the hen
clucking around the henhouse at night
screaming for the eggs
like the nest
ill-fitted for the swollen bird who cannot fly
for wings too long
and body too large to fit inside
and this is why i am me
and sorry
and swollen with pride
i am like ten examples
at once
watching them collide
like broken dinner plates in mid-air crash
boom and bang
crashing as i catacomb into the tile
i should have stayed simply alone longer
for a while
so i am a cemetery of new ideas again today

But Still

I am haunted up the coast
it can't be soon enough
that sand
that gets in your toes
goes back to the side of the sea
and our ship is forgotten
off the reef
and abandoned for a mossy grave
and fish
curious
and interested in the dark deep places
they dwell

I am haunted in the house
it can't be for this long
that sound
that rings like my voice
talks to you still in accidental phrase
when it is for me
or someone else
deserved
with good will
calm
slowly my tanks refill themselves with new things
and light

but still
I am haunted
it can't be for long
and
it can't be soon enough
but still

Every Day

Every Day I Die some
turn some
i get up to the gate
i buy the ticket
i wait
i watch others go by
every one
i wonder to myself if it cares
the hole
going
is it through
i don't
not if it's going to mean something
something to her
and not me
trying to erase a "you"
a her
to me,
i will not miss the swing
false tides and moon
throwing my face against the wall
i violate my own space
struggle
born like that
a closed-open wound
disgusting
and always too soon
i am all this
so i wait
unafraid
lazy in fact and faint
barely a person
barely

skydragon

skydragon
your reflection casts light back into sky-swallowing clouds
rolling and gray
doing inner ear like shapes
inside themselves
there are lights on inside you
people in there
turning them on and off
like skin cells
activating a new tingle
in your metallic body
in your perfect way
standing alone
indifferent
cold
like a fuck-you to the sun and the night
like a drunk
skydragon
off Fifth Avenue
you old whore you fucking crooked face
did you let yourself get that way
from design
or from lack of the energy to stray
because you got tired
and if he crawled over you
in merry ol' England
maybe you might get some sleep
and it's more trouble to be desired
than had
or so you thought
in his hotel room, in his bed
even though you said he wore you down
that rat-face
that scumbag
you let inside
his office empty but his name upon the door forever
wasteful
on your way home somefuckingwhere
wherever that was

PRICE

Chapter 11

chapter IV

Almost Out

i am almost out
ten cigarettes went quick
like that
half a day
one left
with a butt in the tray
i'll smoke that as i write
ok?

i have a face burnt in my eyes
i have a hand burnt into my hand
i have a heart
or what is left of one
a rolling desert
fucked white with sand
and bright
from heat
saturated into the light
in my gills
when i turn into the fish
out of the water tank
into her cup
like a lower-class wish
i am a volcano
i am ready to erupt
a tsunami
smashing into her coast
pulverizing the beach
making toast out of a hotel lobby
nice
with your nose raised and glazed
like a donut covered in salami
so snobby
flying like a witch to an invitational snitch
gathering
pink lights shine above a liquor store
called "the pink elephant"
now THAT's funny
i know those people
their sad dinner food
their reluctant sway
they too

are almost out
we are all
almost out
of something
almost.

Cease Fire

once the fires of hell cease
cease fire
and the smoke clears
that is what i started with
those words today
i stop
looking at your face
or thinking
about your hands
i loved them
i loved your hands
hands
like if they were designed by a god
regardless
of him
an afterthought
when he made them
like a painter
slashing a definitive historical line
across a canvas
as he turned
to discuss the morning news
with an old friend
that was your hands
on
my skin
and
today the sun eats the spaces
between buildings
dogs go crazy people lightly cuss
and the colors
people wear
go thoughtless
because
we have a temperature
and everyone is
aware of their neck
chest and back
for
small patches of wet
salty pools
and

of all days
of any day
as i sit and wait
to leave
for no reason
i
imagine
your hands again
and not the faces of men
they touch now
nor
their long digits fiddling with pens
or thank you notes
or receipts
nor
of them silently at your side
waiting
to dart
into the air
at a party because there is always a party
and how the ends of them will turn in
like claws on an eagle
when
you make that point
when you stress the word
so hard
it bends
then breaks
and becomes
an actual word floating
before us all
hovering in mid-air
for
your mouth made it
and your hands
they
were enough to break a heart
watching them
lie still
across your side
as
you slept
in
those beautiful days

the
future
looks
so
fucked
now

Dream Past This

If you dreamed past this
past this part
with me
you would see the raspberry hollows
marsh-mossed rock
and what my eyes are
those
blue
two
loose
marbles
and surround us, very little light between us
        in the dark spaces
would he like neon outlines
        and you
you would speak "speekahlikah thees"—laughing
        and you
"speekalikah that" as we talked of our original
first or
in my case
lower-class mythology stomping grounds
and i would laugh
like a Southerner does
because
we are taught young to make much fun
of others, despite ourselves,
cobwebbed duck-limbed south
people we are
even when we defect like me
        a defector
        dedicated to an island
        as if to share
        a recreational dream
        or an isolation
        masked
        as a shared dream
my born-cross, every fell pine rocked of its salt
from the air of the coast
my miserable cobblestoned wishes
and that God-forsaken ocean
that sound of doom and chaos
it created

it really brought me to my knees in despair
those forever-nights
BUT
if you dreamed past this part
you'd see me
strawberry-red, laughing so hard
over milkshakes in a diner so bright
so alight with you
or
something, something just like this
maybe waiting, maybe
if i trust my spells of tireless excitement
this city
maybe
if

BubbleGummed

(for Mary-Louise)

You,
You are on that old piece of metal
a heart
on a wire
hanging above the downtown lurch
of a street
blast neon
white light
clatter go the taxis past
feet bruised with suit weight
and rushing
in the screams
i see you
or
i see your name
You
You are on that old piece of metal
spelled out
like that

You,
You stretch out very long
too long even
pale white
littering things on my thoughts
i project across the room
through the windows
onto the hudson
and buildings interrupting
you
with bubblegum things
with hands
to hold my face down
into the fire pit
of night
and
i can feel the light of the moon
in your greasy paws
poster-girl stuff
i think you are a jail
representing what i like

way up there
swung with bulbs
neon blast county fair
white light
broken up upon a star
bubblegummed
and
blazed.

i always knew you could do better

nobody has arms universe size
to reach around us now
that we went
nighttime hush
and
shadow with glitter spots
so
i catch a butterfly in a jar
when i close my eyes
and release it
as i say your name
it's what my doctor
it's what he said to do
might i undo your name
from mine
if for an ever

but i riddled with rainbows like visions
of misspellings and you fixing them
but how i spelled them
made you smile
until you were shipwrecked into me
sunken in
to a hack
because you dreamed me a beach
and i always, under sand, understand
buried my head and feet stuck out
where you live now
someone who isn't me
like this
and i am ok i guess
   i always knew you could do better
than me
anyhow

nobody has arms universe size
to reach into the landfill for my sweaters
you threw away with the stripes
of my blanket, i named, for how lonely
I became
somewhere a seagull hovers over a landfill
and shits on a letter with both of our names

next to a rotting carton of eggs
i try to make myself tea
like you would make that tea each day and
like clockwork at night it would be in a pirate corked glass bottle
but i burnt my arm
and myself
in that moment i became so weak i was 33 years old
and just some crazy man alone
in his kitchen crying
   but i always knew
i always knew you could do better
than me
i always knew that.

What a "Someone Else's" Is

Uh oh,
I think I let someone take me when i was an egg
already cracked
and make me into
something hearty
but flat
facedown against the bedsheets
or sometimes
not even that
Uh oh,
I think I let someone take me when you were not looking
when cracked
yourself maybe
either way
we are ALWAYS theirs for the taking
surely,
if one or both of us is not looking
even once
because we made ourselves that way
surely,
    my insides went from an ocean to a creek
  and no smile is all for real, ever
  since
  i slept with you midday cheek on cheek
  like in the movies
because THAT
"that" just Does Not Happen
  not really
it is just a wish or why would they go through so much trouble
  did you ever think of that?
a wish upon a wall
and eyes upon the wall for having heard of such a thing
or a twenty
with sodas and candy
and silenced cell phones
that is
all but yours
so
so many tears
i am always ruined now no matter
how loud i make my colors
or how hungry

those mouths may be
—it all comes out
eventually
wash or not
and trust me
they see
i am a plate of food left half eaten and belonged
if only ever once to a taker who paid and did their thing
did what they chose and paid
and that,
that is no love
but exactly what and how it is today
and everybody knows
what a "someone else's" is, my love
and I,
my dear,
I am not exactly that
uh oh.

like a werewolf

if i were a vampire
i would drink my own blood so that i would die backwards
or something
do something with black magic
to make eternal life go musical chairs
for a second
and i would have never been here
for you to destroy
with bad checks
written out on good will as payment
of some kind
for love—
bound in the binds
not me
not at this age
not at this time
when i am softer
and
hardly fought
to grow more into something new
when i have barely rested for the dying
to get older
as it is
new and whole or not
like a werewolf
i roam these nights built to destroy
fuzz-faced hairball vampires
or else i will expire
because,
besides that i have to be sober
i have been wishing for a new box of dreams
to project upon the walls of my house
the house of my heart
and soul
but only so you might see it and your eyes
would go back to blue,
vampire,
and the audience would sigh
for i had done a good thing
even i
a creature of the night
you and i

then hugging and kissing under the moon
as the credits rolled by
the projector playing that fill the red balloon
and everyone starts laughing
as they are crying
which is sad
because i will probably eat alone again today
and talk to myself in mumbles like who cares if i am crazy
it might keep others from finding their way in
i do not save the day
or get the girl
like a werewolf.

New Pieces

i am with Y O U dreamer
your red halo in the pillowpile
cottonskin
and all slow slow s l o w
b r e a t h
i am with you.
past tense,
of course.
in the shadow of a green couch
in the back room where we sat
laughing laughing eating
operating machinery
no thought
            the glass floor somewhere shines round your legs firework bulbs
            voices drown out
the bow breaks
the time comes
the time passes
we are alone, or
now, now we are
by ourselves, us
us,
what was that?
my god.

still i am with Y O U dreamer
perhaps i am the deer caught on the gate
fast fast fast horns antlers shake
woodcrack broken gate
burning passed me like ancient kharma
or fate
or dinner hungry miners the bell goes D I N G
and out come the dirty faces
we were here
once
in the arms of the orange-fall-white-lights
and under glass
so with you, dreamer
i am,
that i sleep with my head in that direction still
of the bed
though it will not speak back

or breathe for you
it is a broken mold
cast once
for something new
that just got up and went
just like that
and then
then came spewing us, at least to me
came spewing the confetti of us
only missing
half of this
us
in new pieces

Burn Up

Here's the wind-up, kids . . . no really
i have this amazing funeral idea
hop a spot on a Soviet satellite rocket
after i am dead,
of course
my body in a heat-guarded, air-tight
sarcophagus
made of metal
the mold
my body hands crossed Ra style
with headphones on
mirror shades
striped shirt
paratrooper boots
and hair a fuckin mess
all this
with a flashing red light
that sends my signal and progress
to anyone of interest
as it is let go
in outer space
headed round the moon for speed
and a swift delivery
into the heart of the sun
the return to the light
and
kingdom
if i pulled this off i would still be laughing
now
as time shifts backwards from now
to forward
so,
let's just say i am granted access
i will turn it off, the sun, i will
so you will know
how it felt
to love you
and be thrown away like a dirty rag
vultures
why can't they just glow in the dark
so us boys, we might
might watch out

they eat your eyes first
then the heart
it has the most meat
and
they're schooled and mannered those girls
and rarely go for seconds
so arms out
either way
and douse
here is the wind-up, kids, ready or not
it is time
time to
burn up.

Chapter Eleven

What what what is that ringing in my ear?
they are tearing down another theater
your unfinished works will never see the stage
see the stage
boom
bye bye stage
worst of all I am only thinking of you
writing like a courthouse typist
taking dictation
what do you call them?
and
the world is about to change

can you see that fire under there?
it burns too bright like it had lungs
and too much air
surrounding it up there
this thing with eyes
shrouded in walls
and alibis
I am powerless against you
and your lies and left to die
alone
with my thoughts
which only go "why"
an infinity number of times
and
the world is about to change

it's about to get dark
forever clouded
black and still
crushed and whip-poor-will dust
I can't wait
I can't wait
to file into line
and disappear
into that foggy gate

we will not meet again
I'm afraid the work is done
mine and yours

oh look, there's a party
that's nice, dear
run along
your father paid the bill
and
guess with what
guess

what's that thing you cannot touch?
touch it anyways
a truth to move your hand
born slouched
draped like a drunken game horse
bottled up
half hanging off a cubicle desk
into this word
with meaning
so tough, someone get a violin
and play something
slow
and dim
but don't even dream of a drum
that will
of hers
what is that, pride?
crossed legs
your fingers type
words to him
whoever undoes them then
I will not be there
of course
again
and he doesn't even know his soul is dying
the light just hit him
how fast won't matter
once you like him
enough to give him a piece of rope
and trust me,
he'll start tying
fast as he can
so strange
how I ever saw such a love in someone like you
and
the world is about to change
and

go bankrupt
let it go
chapter eleven now
because then
then
we'll see who is rich
and
who is fucked
for good.

Butterbrains

butterbrains,
gosh,
that is what I am
half man
half beast
I don't listen well
constantly
in search
of more
belief
maybe even tipped like a loaded scale
if the other side were peace
that is mine
my grief
mein grief
I unplugged from the t.v.
started listening
no cars this morning
valentine's day
people
or maybe just one person
slides the noose
firmly
around their neck
and pushes the chair
we lose some
to their hearts
and lack of care
no referee
to intervene
so sad
and serene
but I feel like there are bubbles
you know
enough to fit my bath
at least for me
mid-prayer
to any angel or God
no matter
how great
or distant
that I care

and I wonder if God needs love too
I wonder should I pray for God
that God tolerates us
as small as we may be
but to him
butterbrains,
that is what I am
totally
and finally buying the light
with my faith
not my words
stupid like a river
with three trees
on either end
rocks and streams
branching off into the dim light
of morning
this reads like a trajectory
not a warning
I just am
I just am
you know
beside myself again
not looking
being my own best friend
hairy and praying in a bath
for anyone
butterbrains
me
butterbrains

fuck it all

how wet
you know
she was
for someone allergic to being loved
adored
how much fruit fell from my tree
was astounding
and to think now
how it does not feel empty
you know
my body or heart
from the loss of the feeling of fucking through the love
and the hurt
is strange
I torture myself sometimes
thinking of that silk-shirted thick beer-tongued brat
with a car, a family lineage, and an expensive hat
and what she looks like
when he pulls his dick out
and she lays back
her eyes too blue
to focus on it
you have to be a big kid, they said, to ride the black wave
because it does not respond to love kindly
and would much rather be a slave
and ridden and beaten like a horse
in full jockey
halfway to finish line
and punished
but all this with no wet kisses and no real violence
implied
like when you want the check at a restaurant
and make the "I'm writing something" sign

for a kick
and a stutter
of lost things
gone sailing in the brutal winds of change
and growing old
and wearing out
and rusting
alone

living in hope
like a stubborn kid
allergic to the knowing
love has come and left
silently
without an end
and yet
this springtime scare
it is inevitable
and something inside the gray
it is growing

if the rest of the world were as selfish as you are
regardless of heaven or hell
or an afterlife, where a soul is judged
you would not be here
for your lack of faith
in the service of others
and for what is decent

and the waitress smiles
and goes into her station
where you can't see her
and cries
I am not doing myself or anyone any good on this fucking earth, fuck
fuck it all

giggle

I bet you see me
right now
writing this
and think
"I want that vacuum"
the one on the t.v.
in the window
but
if you knew her
and knew me
would you
you know
want it still
or see
I am going to trace your outlines with my fingers
even though the maid will come
and remove us both
by sundown
this is how it is
I am kind of investigating myself now
in a thick stab
of openings
and I guess
all it took was that look
between
you
me
and this time machine
revolving
around the moon
before
I knew what it meant to feel something again
that didn't
feel like diving through a mirror
or falling through a burning river
I will sleep tomorrow
then awake
and shiver
and be alone again
with only me to fight the dark of day back against that wall
but somewhere
I
will hear you giggle

say something

don't just stand there
say something
say something

27 Steps

Robert stood on the docks, his favorite shirt stained with fish blood, the wire mesh nets behind him, over him like spiderwebs, his shirt sleeves rolled up to his elbows and his arms a boxer's size. At this age a man does not do this type of work, the old men must have thought, as they peeled the gloves from their hands while the younger fishermen dumped the flinching silver diamond-eyed fish into the once-green buckets, now more filthy white. The boats surrounding were older, and beaten alive by salt and war winds and however many times it had been beached for the scraping of the coral. Robert stood on the docks.

His eyes upon the city behind the pier, and the organized messes upon the beach seemed more like chaos to the wanderers and to the fishermen too, probably sometimes, but so did this skyline. And somewhere inside, somewhere, he would find the bookbinder who crafted for him a sheath to protect his words. Twice did his notebooks go down, or so to speak, when sailing through a storm, everyone calm, and aware of each wave only as a heartbeat inside a chest on a busy day.

Some of the writing was damaged, but not really, you could read every word but he was fickle and alone out there. A man is only what he has to say, you know, inside, and that was Robert anyway. From day one. From day one he knew his name. And that was a good spell ago but not exactly forever from yesterday.

"Oh, Robert," his sister's only friend Claudia said, half cheeped or yelped, in her funny voice. "Oh, Robert, I am over here, over H E R E," hand waving madly through the air. As she ascended the foot of the pier.

A simple yellow dress with a handkerchief, slightly orange, tangerine orange, and bright blue eyes also. Not even 25.

"Hello, Fruitface," Robert said, kneeling as he knotted a bag of clothes, a pair of simple black shoes, atop the cloth sack. A dark blue cloth and a small white rope like pair of lines ran directly right and left and his hands, they were huge, with fingernails beaten slightly around the base and only a few of the smaller ones showing signs of being recently bloodied or bruised with blue gold copper–looking wear. His hands were the size of good and bad ideas, like two for one, or separate. Claudia liked them.

"Hello there, sailor, ha, who says that? Right, I mean, it's funny to say that, I suppose, so how are you, or, are you ready to go? We certainly better put a push on it if we want to get a taxi before 4 . . ." Claudia's voice mumbled through, in a steady up-and-down notation, almost a bird's song with words really. And you hear the coffee in her.

"Yes, yes, let's get going. I believe I am as tired as I have ever been," Robert laughed. "How are you, lovely?"

Claudia removed her gloves (she wore gloves, don't ask) and leaned against the wooden telephone pole–sized beam which rung the last few steps of the pier before it hit the concrete mess, a few of them side-by-side impromptu loading ramps, with wet sand (gray) and loose sand (bottle-blond and white) bunched up beside and blowing smoothly over, as the wind was only below the streets above and the roar of the West Side Highway and it could be the traffic maybe that replaced that quiet roar of wind, but you imagined they were making the sound, you thought it would have to be one or the other, but above, behind them, that was a wind of only noise and motion and the bending of time. That is what a person does when they live in there, inside the fault lines of a thousand buildings with as many windows multiplied by however many times.

She leaned her neck back to take in the sun from the simple blue sky forever shining light off the waters, put her hand to her side, and let out a sigh. "Sometimes, Robert," she paused, "sometimes . . . sometimes a woman doesn't need the weight of a man."

Then she turned as she removed her glasses and smiled.

"That day is not today," Claudia muttered through a set of almost shut lips, her mouth as straight as any line.

Robert stood up now from collecting his few things, a simple dark blue cloth bag and a few books to be rebound and covered in plastic or a binding shell. And he smiled, as they together lunged into a laugh, her arm reaching over to his side, and off they jutted like a painter's line up the dull gray colors of the rocks, to the orange burst and light explosions above them, on the other side of the boats, 27 steps up.

Pretty with Laughter Coming

Geologists
are they
dirty people?
tied to rocks. they know equations for what is what.
they probably understand
the rust
under your nails
our nails
Either way this afternoon was too boat-shaped
and
grew sails
and
off I went into
one of my spells
I couldn't sleep
I never do
so well
so
there is thunder now in my fingertips
from orange paint
and I can't tell
anymore
if I should be tired or faint
for
the rain outside
that blue
and
the coffee I made
it's all
a
long
series of days anyways
and
I am happy
to
imagine a new set of legs moving
soon
where
I will not be walked over
or
trampled on again
like

so many rocks
on a mountain
made
of
bubblegum eyes, cotton insides
and
just a touch of man
in balance
in a wind
by
a single stick
in the sand
and
now we are on this beach so it is up to someone else
or I am for the taking in
taking home
or
left for the waters
to
carry me in
back
into the
dark black of the sea
where you cannot see your hand
two feet
just black
and
I'm hoping
I see
the shoes
when the hand comes down to brush me off
and hear a giggle
before that
it is not yet afternoon
and
there are plenty of
hours
in the day left
and
I saw something pretty
with
laughter
coming

By the Words

something funny happens
in the heat
under the fireball out west
I go to light my morning smoke
just one
in the morning
not one a.m.
a single stick of wake-up blast
to match my cup
of muddy frenzy
and I can't see the flame
for the light
   a coyote nest is in the brush
   is it a nest of bones or paper?
   maybe debris
   from shopping gone wrong
   or a lost
   canyon sweater
   turned article of questions
   that part I don't know
this is still me
and I am here but I am half dreamed
gassy and all man in the morning
cocked and loaded
and stumbling like a drunk
until I light that fuse
and submit myself
to the word
the morning word that is just this
   a desert hides beneath the surface
   its tree its flower its highway
   congested like a face
   of a child
   melted into mexican and american indian
   dreamlike where television comes from
   and I only see her with others
   in the last part of my slumber
   after I wake up once
   but decide for christmas again
   I will go back to bed
   to give my body a new present of rest
   and peace

something funny happens
when I know I am now awake
even in the last bit
of my dreaming
I see you
and I choose your laugh with others
I pick ones, I know their names
always james, always zack
some hack
with a bank account and a phone
that rings like a rooster cooing hens
it is how I undo the ribbon
on the boxes of pain you wrapped for me
under a tree of pain
my mother planted
a long time ago
and just for me
   but I can't carry this for you
   my arms are tired
   my heart wasted
   and a new body makes my wish
   separates the fan from blade and grill
   my fingers won't go in
   on the new watch
   I am meant to heal
   which I do
   but from her laugh and her eyes
   one at a time
I hear you say "no regrets" and I die
over and over
a single stick of wake-up blast
to match my cup
of muddy frenzy
and I can't see the flame
for the light
   so
I light that fuse
by the guesses we have in a single soul
and submit myself
to the word
the morning word that is just this
and pray
a prayer of getting up and being ready
to release the payload
of just

one more day
if that is all I have
this is how we pray
once we pass
through fire
if we do not pass at all
or only for one last time
in a stumbling block of dreaming
far away
in a memory
in a new way
locked down in a jail of old questions
and
time
then I am alive now
one by one
by the words

A Book of Spells

How to make a Book of Spells
is not the question exactly
is it,
but
How might one make a spell to outlast his mouth
and for the thing
inside the face
that makes it spit words like machine-gun fire
or
explosions needed
4th of July–esque
or just a spinning
and a self
How might one make that book
is what
and why
and
I guess maybe everyone should and we would know more
about why
why
why you say I hope you fail
as if by sharing I am trying to win a something
or
beat you to the metal where the apples float
because
once you open your mouth
and start bobbing
we are all an ass
whether or not
we are publishing
and
that is why
and how
Now

Poetry Is a Zombie

Poetry
What is that really
It is the closed Mall Where Zombies Feast on Brains
In my t.v.
When I lie in bed at night
And should be thinking about sex
Poetry
Outmoded
Taken Over and Ammended Beautifully
By Hip-Hop Culture
Made Useless by Napkin Commercials
Poetry
Dead Languages
It works for This
Did You Know
There are people out there, some women
Who read poetry
Who read
And who live by the word for lack of the touch or the word
Or someone to touch
Or that these books
Are
Much better than firewood
I don't know anymore
Really
I am very very stoned
And it is mid-afternoon
And I am talking to you
And I don't know
Who
Or
Where you are
This
Is
Poetry

Cinderella

Cinderella
between the legs where the balls are
that's the wink
that's the fucking subway rattle
so fuck you
and see it from the balls
and the place
where the fire is and where the hot comes from
because you are cold
and your fences are brittle
and the wires look a mess
and the chickens and animals run loose
out your sad gate
then tell me about that music in my mind
when you whistle out of step
tuneless in time
with a feathered cap and a gown
and a seeded palm
to seduce the ships from the safe waves
into the rocks
with your wicked lighthouse lights
shining black on water
in that fucking night
I am too young for this
I am too old for that
I am too weak for you
between my legs where the balls are
my battleships are pirated
my seas triggered with anger
and the wrath
of the day of the dogs
so cast your wicked eyes from mine
and be a child
but not to me
because I am further now than gone
and your feet give you away
with your dark heart path
and those shoes
so wrong
you are weaker than those drinks
with those girlyboys
fruit, seafoam, glass, and umbrella

chase it to the bottom of the pile
it's trash
and I am glorious in my natural bottomless rage
and far too clean
Cinderella

Tonight, We Ride . . .

Tonight,
Tonight we ride into the collapses and see
Bring a torch
Bring a light
and a rod
for testing if the ground is water-signed
and
bring a book of mythology
be mythos bound or not
and
let's go underground
on
these imaginary horses
we cannot name them
for they fall
easily
in such tremendous battles
with the army of spiders
and rats and
whatever that huge scary thing is over there—whatever you
call that
Tonight
Tonight,
We cast an arm above the water the size of what is too big
and too high up
like above the stories once falls
and laughs it off
even in anomalies at kentucky college keg parties
But really to be honest
there is much slowing down
slowing down
going on
I have seen it all around
even the dreamers, they look tired now
as those drugs, even
those drugs, even
do not work like they once must have
even if you wanted to
and
forget that
even the dreamers now are tired
and they,

they are the ones alongside me
as we say
TONIGHT
and shout that ever so naïve, us in the middle years
it comes off childish
but it is just pre-old
because
surely you see how the aged say and laugh like children
who have seen
right
TONIGHT
we ride
but first
we must nap
and
think
about
all that

53 and 38

it rained a little today
and ivy went hush
said can't you see we're busy growing up things
and you're thinking out loud, stop talking to us
something in the news
bout how they moved a statue of Ramses
cause it was deteriorating from car exhaust
I don't remember where they were taking it
probably closer to the pyramids   XXXXXXXXXXXXXXXXXXXXXXXXX
I started reading something about these fishermen   XXXXXXXXXXXXXX
and a story about Picasso and his little dog Lump
a dachshund from Germany, no really, Picasso was from Spain of course
although they didn't live in Spain
they lived in the Villa de California on a hillside in Cannes
there was something about Mozart too
at the bottom of the page
it was bold and italicized but it only said his name
I could never pick up a drink again
without feeling poisoned, I'm spiritually allergic but whatev
what kind of god do you have? do you like plays?
the wedding went on for 5 straight nights
and 5 straight days
five days straight
he was 53 and she is 38

c'mon, let's go

I don't know
what I was thinking
I guess I just got sad
for a while
I was just afraid of being loved
and feeling good
being listened to
listening
understanding
and being understood
I don't know
I just wanted to be alone
alone with somebody there
so I wouldn't get scared
I didn't really like myself
am I saying too much?
I hope not
if anybody feels that way
and it helps
then I will sing to you
while we are here
without a touch
some things were made to be felt

so go outside and watch the stars come up
don't get caught up in way that it's designed
it isn't for us
to analyze
it's up there for us to feel
like somehow
everything that got touched
turned to the light
and I can hold that thought for long enough
it makes the pain disappear
and if there isn't anything left
in the fight
throw in the towel
take off the gloves
and leave the ring
and go outside and listen to the sky sing
look at all the stars lighting up everything
darkness isn't anything

but the space in between the light
the light is so real
and it's where you are from
so let's go
c'mon

The Wind-Up

are there any volunteers by choice in the ways of the heart
who grow up strong like their fathers and sprout dreams
to be piano movers
or is it just something you inherit for need of
replacement not genetics not something in somebody's bloodstream
and is there anyone who moves those things
who gets lazy on break and twinkles at the keys
who gets strayed from the day's work and carried away
and ten years later is sweating moments before he hits the
stage at carnegie hall
after being nervous for days, knowing his parents are gonna be there
and he feels pressure to play it good, considering
it was them that told him he was throwing it all away
on a shot in the dark, with a sure thing right in front of his face
it's 5:21 and my plants are in
and phone is ringing and the nighttime is coming.

Land This Bird

just below me
the crystal city my home forever
lonely or not
manhattan island
place of ghostbusters and drunk riots
is someplace downstairs of this plane
I can feel it
my bones recharged
my body satanic almost and my kidneys blah
from pressure
and klonopin
god
if I were a drunk still I would drink it dry tonight
snort it end to end
call everyone
over and over
beginning to end
in the blackened and brown of the cobblestoned parts of
that town
that fucking box of magic money too much honey that you
all hate
mainly though,
I'd come home to a magic brew
a tea she made
that I loved
and that was her way of telling me
so I knew
boy, how it calmed me so
to lose a lover is the worst of it
but to feel the energy of new places
and lose it
and lose it ON PURPOSE
you know, to be fully american about the loss and pain
that is plain ol' living, baby
and I live in new york
in the borough of manhattan
another bored, overpaid
dentist
I listen to black metal on my headphones and dream of
when
they land this bird so I can smoke and be sad again
perfectly alone

and in love
with a girl named (   ) . . .
who is so gone
I don't even know where she lives anymore
no love lost
for the lost boys
we ride tonight
I ride

Quicksilver

the back of the hand, as it moves across the air
in strike patterns
giving new definitions to light
fingernails
or webs
it is this motion that moves the notes of the day
as I do not count
in my head
but sit
silently and pray
for
a
destiny
and a fate
beyond the glare of such dim phrase and labored breath
and tolerance
when considered
some might die poor
some might die rich
but
the body is the body
and
when the earth is parted
it's nothing but a ditch
it's what you left
that
builds the tower or not
draws the tears
of joy on the face of a hope
not
tolerances and aggressions of time and ability to cope
tie the knot
at the end of the rope
if you must
or turn
and
while you can
fill every heart as your own full of laughter loud as gold
and
passion
quick as silver

Me, Minus Simple Dream

minus simple dreams
I don't mind the teapot and Dolphy and the cliché
because
I sit up here in stacks of books and few clothes
and
some good old shuffle-clutter
to keep me saturated
at all times
even
when I close my eyes
and
my god
that is such a fucking sometimes
such a fucking sometimes
that
thing
sleeping
but you know the kind
where
youwake
hairsamess
and
the yawn feels like you are coming on her chest
I mean
refreshed
I don't know why I say things like that
where I got a mouth like this
but in here
it feels
alright
I guess
because I am two years sober today
and that is not poetry
dear reader
but
a willingness to confess
that those nights
man
they feel ever so slightly lonely
like you
were the star
of your own black-and-white movie

ABOUT
nothing
but the ticking of a clock that should be quiet
but it is so
so loud
and
then
SCREEEEEEEEEEEEEEECCCCCHHHH
goes Nettie the tea kettle
reminding me
a lady is in the house
if only
a
porcelain one
a different porceling one
anyway
a kettle
to
warm my stomach
make it settled
and
like candles
it's a home
when you take your shoes off
breathe in
and light
a candle
outside
the
skyline
is a crown
above a grid struck
with strangers
stuck
to their own skin
and battles and
I don't like it when
we exchange unneeded glances
I
am here
out on the street
I think
to myself
at night
to

be alone
do you see laughter, a woman carrying flowers and balloons?
no
just me
so
I don't mind the teapot and Dolphy and the cliché
because
I sit up here in stacks of books and few clothes
and
some good old shuffle-clutter
to keep me saturated
at all times
even
when I close my eyes
and
my god
endless
me
like
I was
—txt mssng—
and
procrastikissing my own records
asses
perfect
I guess
minus simple dreams

Tea

Once in a while it becomes time
time to paint over the face
one brush stroke at a time
until it's gone
then it's really summer again
and the ice cubes melt into the glass
on the porch
into the tea
until they are gone and the drink is ruined
and nothing in the Bible can save you. now.

My Price

my price
is the prize of the bed
and the high of the fuck
and that sucks
but that's my price
and
what it costs
because
I am a believer
and it's what I do
whether or not
you do
because
beyond that gate
is something new
god
or something forgot
I am
just like that
and my price
is high
like the sun on the metal
of the beams
of a skyscraper
punching holes in the sky
or legs
at the foot of a car
steering it
through canyons
my body wants to
enter in
righteous like an angry shepherd
flocked with a messy white gang
his own
to lead her into her room
and just bang
on that door
for laughs
is what a love is
and that
is my price

i hate myself

"i hate myself
now
fully
which is a step
at least
in some direction
because
i must have deserved it
i must have
and
i don't care anymore
if
the light dies
and
we all
drift
into
nothing
i
deserve
nothing
so
maybe
just
cast me off
with a
push
because
i
am not
afraid
of the falls
not afraid
i
just
wish
it
would
stop
i
wish
i

could
shut
it
off
rip
it
out
of
my
fucking
chest
not
even
to sleep
just
not
this"

17 Poems a Day

if I said I wrote 17 poems a day
at most
and 3 at the least
why would you believe that
for a minute
while your eyes are resting
on each space between the words
and letting the letters bleed
inked
into a pool of white
I wonder
is it me you really hear in here
or are your eyes
unattached to your ears
but to your heart
loyal
and like a dog
hard to lose
if I said I saw the entrance into heaven in a dose
of over-the-counter cold flu stuff
and I meant it all the way
would you go there
go there
with me
or would you just sink,
I pretend I am the antarctic and I found a glacier
and
look at what happened now

OK?

I keep the language simple
I tell myself, "it is to be more like e. e. cummings"
but it is because I am afraid
I will misspell
and
that is why
I have no unfinished work
oh well
you feast on my bones anyway
silent
far away
long before we are this way
reader
your hand here
holding this page
I wish it
were
not more
like my face
hidden
but
like a sketch artist
it begins
and
it ends this way
with nothing but the line
and
a directional line
pointing which direction
a real one might
but
with words
then I say something about myself to reveal a truth like,
"I have never liked being alone
but I am afraid of others
their colorful faces
words
and forgiving
it opens a darkness in me
something
like the past
if it were made of coarse fabric

cotton with thorny vine
and shadow
in a room painted all white
with no light
but one
above and far far
too bright"
so
if you see the sign
or the lights outside
it's because
I am
becoming
something
again
and again
and I liked you when you lived in michigan
(you might never have lived there,
even once,
but pretend)
and
if you opened the door
it wouldn't matter
most of me
it never gets in
I stay
inside
even when I am outside, even then
even then
but
if you wanted to break the lock
on a man
know that it is through his weakness for good shoulders
that do not cave
and keep the language simple
and
maybe it would be two digits
then maybe
we're one away
but
my heart is a defensive lineman
for my
ability to
shake you like a christmas tree
on

no holiday
but for the heat and a chiseled light
lazy on a cotton sheet
in the
middle of the day
my
head is full
of fantasy
reader
fantasy
is how you and I
we got this way
even
if
you hate me
and
this
we now, in this moment
will never
separate
what
a
gyp
right?
or
is it
ok?

TOMORROW HAPPENS

8

Joy

When you say a thing that I write too much
I dream myself a thousand-plus
more books I wrote myself
and imagine them in a swinging stack
fainting
and collapsing onto you
as they crush your bones
in the name of art
in the name of american idealism
in the name of the future
because
fuck you and your sleeping wordless criticism
and
that path before me is lit with possibility
and lore
and my cup is not full because it is not a cup
it is a life
it is a heart
and me
I am trying to show you something
about yourself
not me
that a person can do anything
and
that is what hope is
so,
with all due respect,
fuck you if you dismiss this
because it is a process
and
I accept
if you discount what it has to say
but if I draw a line
and say
what have you done today
be prepared
because while you are sleeping
I am with the sunlight
and the life
and joy
joy will rise in the names

Orange-Burst

Orange-Burst knows—
full-tilt knows, bumper car sparks knows
beach bum salty hair in eyes—knows
that I am here
under it.
Made of sunlight
Orange-Burst is
and all "Nun-ya-business-esque"
because it rained
and
I have a thing for lamps.
Lights—lightbulbs—signs with lights—
you name it—
I have a thing.
Not digital or laser though.
Working ones—
Ones where you have to be careful or
DAMN
that small piece comes off the rods
those tiny metal legs
extending up
and the connection is lost forever
I'd cry if they turned off the Chrysler
cry baby tears
but maybe I wouldn't know
sometimes
sometimes I can't get out of bed.
I spend almost every waking hour absolutely alone.
Orange-Burst knows.
I love it.
It laughs
out loud with light
as a heaven might
and
a man needs friends at 6 a.m.
and I don't work anywhere
but here
so
Orange-Burst—
off we go.

Fast As Fuck

Maybe all you meant to say was,
"gosh, what a waste to see a good man lose his faith"
and that is why
when I got lost
and you knew,
you told me to write,
because I was very sad
and a sad man is a sad thing
too sad for words
maybe
but his own

so
While they thumb for a dollar now
and loose change
when the offering plate comes around
silver
and charity-bound
I am dumping collections
entire passages of a life
because
I dug the ditch
I roofed the house
I bagged the groceries
I got fired
I sung a song
I broke myself
I broke others
and now
now I want to be, NO, BEAT that idea
that a man does not change
also
like an athlete
or a machinist
I want to know how much my spirit can lift
how fast a heart can go
and
how slow a world can turn
when frozen by the violent twists
of a dream
gone thuder-tornado-thuNder tornato
even when I misspell

so
Maybe all you meant to say was,
"gosh, what a waste to see a good man lose his faith"
but I heard you
a bunch of ways
now after-while a buncha ways
and
this is the work
and
the work will not change
unlike me
fast as a fucking scene
inside a t.v.
the size of a galaxy.

Pay Up, and Let the Kids Play You Sissy

It looks like the mirror-house was glass
. . . "fuck"
the rumbles must be low
to be grumbles muttered
because a truth was told
and stomachs were hungry
not yet lunch
and there was a bunch of shit on about war
war
fuck that
go to war, kill others, yourself, whatever
for "safety"
but I have never felt safe around anyone
who wanted to kill me
or whom
I thought might die needlessly
all that blood
and this feeling we have a soul and there might be a God
in fact
that there might be a rather large presentation
scientific
mathematic
ready behind us,
whatever made our parents
and you know
whatever also made them love and then laugh
fuck
take baths and talk
and make us,
it might be a bad idea to forget you did not measure you
and cut you out of a cloth
and seed yourself in a field of flesh
and fill your veins
which spider-hatched
into a nebula
of tangible webs
before you were even given a name
and declare yourself a God
who punishes
because
and if only this
because

if one stands behind you and after you
imagine his legion
and in your slow-ass monday-morning mind
imagine what darkness
falls under that kind of light
and
remember
soon it will be collection day, either way
and you,
you are what you will be using
when that receipt is handed to you
and someone will pay
ok?
good.

How Spirits Sail

Winter is so fucking over
so fucking over
in here
so last year

I don't have time for you
but love you now
love you still
but removed myself

Intensive care unit typewriter
station on full alert
maybe manic but harmless
and less hurt

Pain can be taken from a place
like in a heart
in its last season
and moved to the knuckles

Hands in the dirt getting way dirty
digging into something
looking for evidence
of life in circles

I stand still and watch me
I revolve perfectly like a planet
inside a system of myself
and release a faction

I gang myself up sort of
because those colors on a dress
and the life under it or outside
is boozy and makes me yucked

Nobody in this place is even aware
of who is borrowing
from where
who is touched and by what

And that whole thing is madness
if you know you are the name

or the other hand connected
to a life inside a desired light

With eyes like yours and a mouth
and ears and arms and legs
and worries and fellowship
raised on shores you did not see

Because, we got here separately
that is how it works
how spirits sail.

Fuck That Noise, Jimmy Shoetaps

Let's go up and down
like me
and my moods, or yours and someone else's too
and see if we can build some rollercoasters
no seagulls ever got to sit on
for the clattering rails
of words and heartbeats
all in perfect time
with the wave
and then the next wave
as it crashes into our beach
where we go
not always together
still
our electric park of thought
and
you know, fuck it
ride 'em all
at least once
or twice
for the laughs.

otherwise
the dust will gather
and on the metal
rust will settle
and I'll be up here fixing this shit
forever
and
you know,
fuck that noise, Jimmy Shoetaps.

Asshole

What an asshole.
Somebody was born today and you went and built a boxing arena.
What an asshole.
Sure, poetry and art are certainly not charity but if YOU built it
and
it's your wallet that gets lined with unicorn feathers
or you were in a position to TEACH not LEAD
and you
showed a child it was possible to bleed
then when that First Punch goes out
shouldn't YOUR FACE be the one?
huh?
Is that how it oughta be,
for the balance to belong to the floor
and to set an example
before you have to even the score . . . ?
You don't care, do you?
No.
So you will now be happy and certainly sleep easy and of course
get fucked royally
but if by other royalty
still . . .
What an asshole.
What an asshole you are,
swallowing yourself in shit.

Garbage Scepter

    Sour Crystals form
and the kings
the kings of the alleys and NOT the streets
the streets outside them
hold their staffs
their scepters
and loot
in sack cloth
to reckon what is theirs
and by their staff
they draw a day
and they draw a night
and we know
we who are not of the living in those boxes of garbage cans
we know
this is their kingdom.

Old Flowers

Old flowers
Break like eggs
in a rented room
with a slow bed
This church rising up
like old men
surrounded by houses
all new like children
With a rain-blasted steeple
fit for vampires
Christ
it makes me sick
and my stomach screams
because it isn't working anymore
like my skin was crawling with bugs
I cannot see
interrupting me
and my shitty dreams
Apples, bananas, and pears in my green glass heart
rot quietly along to a beat
my legs crossed
my typing foot
banging inside the desk
from my wild typing foot—feet—
tired from over-sleep
with a mouth full of smoke and rose petal
tea and eyes following an electric tower
someplace over the water
the car swings back and forth wildly
minus driver
or a road to guide her
I tell lies to get inside her
if only to turn the key
to an off position
and let it happen—sparing somebody
Ten days ago the water went
into the hole where it sits
like an entire city arranged
on a dirty dinner plate
on a tray made of clay turning dirt
from humidity and hurt
for broken men who hurl with knotted shirts

stinging themselves like bees
looking into mirrors
the image of an enemy
someplace in the middle millionties
with their legs tied
and wasted lipstick girls laughing their wallets off
turning money into bags
barely between the cars,
rushing,
glassy like the sun was coming out on repeat inside
but not really
with electric wombs
those rooms were made for sleeping
not research for alibis not worth keeping
star-lined and straight
like a military bed
at 8 a.m.
there are no coincidences, said my friend
who bathes in light
but joined a cult by accident one night
outside
streets on streets on streets
like orgies
for starving feet
a picture of what is mine wrapped up in her mother's arms
above the light
which happily
descended from me
as I too dwelt
lower
before it rose
and it is now always turned on
All-Fucking*night
and me
I break like eggs in a rented room
with a slow bed
I break like eggs
or old flowers
damn
fuck
pity
shame
I will never be mine
for the never being yours
or ours.

Summer

summer is a state of mind
a smelly fish
no meat
all scales
that television of yours
has harpoons
and they breach the whale

your sea
an angry field of static
disconnected from the door
I see the outside
from the inside
but go noplace
near there anymore

landfill is a sky
sky is full of swallows
filling your cup
poison
how do you even spell that
cleaning your plate
thoroughly
everything you do, so perfect and pretty
and never showing up
for the always being late

this place is empty kind of
sans love—home-esqueness pose
without you
I look at the lights I hung
I see the outside of my apartment
but from below
not above

and I see traffic way too heavy
from mistakes
and words used
turned like iron weights on ankles
and me
inside like too many bodies in the trunk
to hide

us living

but summer is a state of mind
and I am going
and willingly
forever
so say goodbye to this me
while I am still yours
before the dirt comes out from under my nails
and I no longer feel shitty
or
beyond the reach of God.

Whatever Makes Her Happy

I sat with her in a movie theater
midday
friday
falling asleep
someplace between my seat
and her shoulder
with clouds passing in the frame
since that day
things have never been anything worse
but not the same
days are born
they revolve
but they do not change
—eternity is here—
—and here—
Our soda is too big for us
Our popcorn might as well be on fire
because it is anywhere but in her mouth
my mouth
christ my mouth
or anyone else's inside this place
inside them
she or I
replaced by another shadow
or shadowy face
and
My clothes are dirty
My mind is not in charge
I had a few reservations
in several areas of interest
but I am the ticket
and I turned the plane around
I didn't show
I just didn't.
Inside you I have every one of you,
demonic assholes tearing and screaming
the housing projects come down
like a video
no posse
no cars
and the women in the lower districts laugh
and taunt us as we go

because the way I talk is like gunfire
and I am fractured with loud parts
army clothes
and my face is loud
violent crowd sound loud
and spitting vowels
this is all a bit much
and confusing
and
well
whatever, man, whatever it takes
whatever makes her happy.

We're the Worst

the wrong side of worst
is
I draw lines
between my enemies
and my friends
and
they intersect so much
I can't see their faces
for the bends
in the book
and what a bath break
took
because you're all way too much
and lovely
but also
just yuck
yuck
gross
the moon plays with a ball of yarn
it tells me jokes
tells jokes also to the yard
dogs go ape-shit
and in the pile of garbage
they roll
snort
and then get up begrudgingly
and go settle down
in a lie
under a tree shadow
fuckers
lucky and pure
in their madness and devotion
and without doubt
so noble a thing
but when living
so pure
minus all that second-guessing
and congestion.
I do not talk about how I feel
so much as I talk about
that I am feeling—"something"
but I dunno what fucking what

really
it's so nonspecific
it talks a lot of shit but doesn't back it up
if I planted something
not the evidence in a coat
but a tree
maybe it might slow something else
everything being perfectly balanced
still I blush
when I get the feeling
a woman is thinking of a saddle-up
forgive me but
I mean,
I got the ticket for me
for us

For Charles

Today is Thursday, Charles,
and I had that old dream again.
I bet it was something like your drinking problem.
You can never admit it
or let it go
so you glorified it
until it wasted you
and your possibility
and you died
right after people started looking like horticulture
and whatever.

I bet God made you join a rollerskating league
I bet you hate it
I bet it's all men too
an all-men rollerskating league
so you don't get any ideas
and besides
rollerskating is a bag of funballs, Charles
and you
they put you in the movie store on the day you passed
in all your drunken glory
and you
you were a good writer
and you saw things
and they were messed up
but they didn't have to be
and those docks
by the swampy pier
they aren't meant for learning
but for ships
cargo
and
the sea.

Today is Thursday, Charles,
and I had that old dream again.
But you are still asleep
and will be forever
and I wish
I wish you could wake me up one more day
to cry

and write a brief note
and leave it on the refrigerator of the world
that you were sorry
and that you really were just scared
and loved too much.
Goodnight, Charles.

No Movie Tonight

Just tonight, walking home I thought,
Maybe I will treat myself to dinner and a movie
but I got cold feet
and I just couldn't
For all that walking down the aisle alone again
For all that unnecessary static I feel
watching grouped shadows before me
side by side
taking it all in together
it does not remind me of her anymore
but it does remind me of me
desperately alone
and
there is just no one
no one
not a soul with a match to relight that fire
and I'm terribly afraid it is in no way an over-exaggeration
but a fact.
You can feel that stuff from this altitude of 33.
I can see the fast-action valley below of youth.
How merciless and warring always
teeth-gnashing war machines, but all pretty and dumb
colliding
and at this height
well
one must saunter on toward the summit
or what point was it anyway
if for stopping now
to find the peak
and know a measurement of a single light
inside this machine of mine
which keeps growing hair
breaking down
and
capable of the longest of sighs
as darkness surrounds.

What If

slice it any way you like
be it a loaf of homemade bread
or a block of cheese

I like it when the mail comes
I open the box one-armed
with a string I keep tied to my belt loop
on its end a gaggle of keys
and there
there is your magazine

we don't finish them
but we try
us youngins or under 40
but as instructed by our elders
we stack them neatly
in our bathrooms or our sitting rooms
or wherever a window is
that gets the most light
for reading them later
under the reflected brick thrown
unnatural light
and
EVEN when you make a funny cover
about politics
some of us don't mind
or even understand
because
in the front pages our poets speak
simple and condensed into phrase
and it is as if at once
I learn each time
to understand a world of hearts
one must focus on a single beat
its flow
and be silent and in the know
what courage it must take
to be at ease enough to expose a truth
single and fit for a feast
of your offices
overstacked with the words of us dreamers
trying our best

to be clever
in the way we use words
when they rhyme and repeat
or not
but
slice it any way you like
if it made it in,
there is a bit of dancing standing fits
when you open the box
and your submission
somehow
against all odds
made it in.

Electric Nothings

Am I still a country mouse
If forever now
I boxed me up
and shipped me up north
and
gave my heart to a city-style dream?
or
am I not a geographical thing?

Am I still a Southern pie
If long past baked
I boxed me up
and was overlooked
for
people here eat mostly cake
and
remember when Johnny Carson used to do that thing
that thing
where you playfully end up
riddled with the whipping cream
interrupting a blush
as it fell onto a suit
from a smiling face?
Am I still?

Because I feel like electric nothings
most days
and find myself engulfed in measurements
my soul fastened to my shoes
my shoes the counterweights
and
I don't feel like I belong much here
or there or not
any more than anything flickering
digital
that a spilled glass of something
could make forgot
gone too
like a season well spent.

This is how we go about it now
now that the curtain and the cast

are simulcast
before and after intermission
with all of us mid-bow
to empty house crowds
and
my body tells me something LOUD
"hey, mister," it says
you are yours
so
I let the words take me where they will
and marry each morning
that clicking sound
far from electric nothings
and south.

War Is Awful

That gun,
That suit,
That thought,
"aim . . . then shoot"
How'd you do it?
What'd I miss?
I kill cockroaches
sure thing, man
I never miss
Well, that's a lie
But what the hell
They invaded
So why not try?
Why not?
Is that how it goes?
That gun,
That suit,
That thought,
"aim . . . then shoot"

Someone made that thing
lust or love
directed by the hands
and silence above
below a floor
not sheets and bed
but rapid miracles
reproducing
like light orb circles
dropping from words
meant only once
for ears now yours
once your mother's
surrounded perhaps
by careful doctors
and a nurse
plus plenty of hot water
and your tears,
all miracles
considering the lists
everywhere
talking "End Is Near"

take this, take that
to calm your fears,
fix you, not IT
like you were a world
funny, but not cute
you're not
so
That gun,
That suit,
That thought,
"aim . . . then shoot"
How'd you do it?

Fuck You, Mister Know-It-All

Sometimes I tell myself,
"Fuck you, mister know-it-all"
but I know I'm right anyway
so I don't talk to myself
for like, seven days
because
I am an asshole
an asshole with a big fucking mouth and also
I am trapped by multicorns
several of them
not to be confused with unicorns
who are also assholish, like swans
beautiful but will fuck with you,
NO multi-fucking-corns,
which are just downright,
um,
nasty, yeah, nasty and awful mean
so you know,
next time you get mad at yourself
think about this
or me
and feel free to keep smiling
and walking on through it
because,
well, what am I even saying here
who am I to tell anybody anything
I dunno shit about anything
my life is a fucking mess
"fuck you, mister know-it-all"
I would tell myself right now
but I'm busy
I'm busy being a poet
or whatever
infinity
plus
whatever makes it impossible to retort
I get the last word here
always.

Sand Sea Tide

I wish it were sea spirits—joining me to the ocean of sadness
or static tides filled with anger and depression—my own faults
sea spirits, green sun-glinting eyes
skin like scales, every color in them
when they moved ever so, standing upon
the beach, with merlin's staff
but I am simply crazy
and me
my loneliness, which I spell so well
is killing me
off
like a crushed bug under a nice set of heels
I am surrounded by misery
and my boat sets sail
and we drift
into that fog
where I shall never see your face again.
sand
sea
tide
when I ask you to take my breath away
what I mean is,
forever
for-fucking-ever

My Watch Hates You

Dear Time,
Fuck You,
I used to get wasted and stand at the edges of buildings
not for show, there would be no one anywhere
not fried style
not even a stranger
and I would know I was wasted when I hung over the side
because naturally I am afraid of heights
that's when
when I would snort a speedball off my hand
you know that place
between your first finger and thumb
that's where you snort them from
I would buy coke
and buy heroin
both powders
and premix
and put them into little pieces of paper
which I would hide in my jean jacket pocket
very small
and I was like a magician
I would pretend to wipe my nose
the way anyone would with allergies
mid-lunch with someone
and I would drop the line into a linen napkin
or just a plain one
and I would snort them
all day
all day and night
but at night eat at least two sedatives
and one painkiller
then get wasted
wasted as fuck
and when the darkness filled me up all the way
I'd find a quiet ledge
and I would try to accidentally fall off
I did this for at least 6 years
I miss it
not the drugs
but whatever else that was, but I don't do that anymore
now I work myself to death
that is my new punishment for myself

and because
during that time at the end
I lost you
I lost you there, I guess
I lost you.
so
Dear Time,
Fuck You
and
watch this watch this watch this watch this and watch this watch this
watch this and watch this
Asshole.

Forget It

slowing hands at ends of stems
pedals
arranged white, purple.
cornrows like directing orbs
of orange/tangerine blast
over a silent
waterfall that is you
and
forget it.

marsh lands toxic dump radioactive
semi-truck
spills toxins, fire, a wreck
fire explosives and up and
down and up and down
so afraid and insanity-bound
glacier
that is me
so
forget it.

Fruit Gets a Lot of Still-Life Action

sit still,
no,
you fucking sit still,
dialogue
between a camera
and
a bowl of fruit
it's tired
it's been there forever
and the set is exhausting
it's tiring work
getting too much love
isn't it?
so it starts to give
the lights are too much
the hours are too long
and the orange is more brown
now than yellow and red
mixed
and the green of the apricot
has softly fizzled out
nodded off in its chair
a sitting bed
in a green bowl
on a table
with large hands moving the pieces
round and round
a race against the clock
time always wins
the cameraman just forgot
for they are driven
driven by madness
against a time
and
the world stops
they think
when you isolate it
small enough
it fits into a frame
but it is a trick
to make you think
that fruit gets all the action

it does not
it dies behind the colors
in the darkroom
and
is nothing,
zero
so move, soldier, move
winter is coming

Aplomb

since nobody is listening,
I will sing this
aplomb
aplomb
I'm singing that song
but I am not dignified
without dignity
I am alone
and no one is listening

this is MY hillside,
my right and left
sky and tree line barren
white canvas
north and south
devoid of color
listless
totally shut-mouth

since nobody is listening
I will sing this
over myself
over myself
and the thump of my own heart
kicking my chest
beating it
with its blood-fist
aplomb
aplomb
aplomb
aplomb
aplomb
I am alone
I am alone
and
no one is listening

Do Not Loan Your Heart to Women

if you raced me home
you would end up
in the woods
woods—white
silent
and
scary
but you know that now,
you know

as we watched the clouds break
into a single hole
like an eye
over the hudson those lines
light beams
they shot the blue to hell
and shrapnel fell
in puddle swallows
every-fucking-where
and you knew,
you knew I was lost as a ghost is
but fully here
body, soul, and bone-whole lost

that's why you told me about the boys
the boys you have on a line
and that problem with collecting them
like I would agree
and say,
"oh, me too, I have a list"
but I do not
my legacy is just ruin
and a rot
someplace in my throat
my heart couldn't find
so the words forgot
so I asked you something easy
and said,
"shall we make our way back into the city?"
of course, you said, and then
we went

If you could race me home
up those beams
you'd have to go
made of light
but changing so fast
they forget where they go
and dissolve
like a crypt
of tombs
into a past
where we are not
because
and I am saying this loosely,
I will not love again,
for I have learned

Dreams, God, Albert, and Disappointment

Albert wakes God up (again) and God is pissed,
but then laughs
and makes tea
tea for two
and they sit by the bay window
and God speaks
and Albert, grinning, says, "hmm"
and not much else
and when he talks
it isn't in a germanic drawl
no
they speak one language
Angelica
which sounds like a puppy barking
about nothing in particular
like an animal sigh
and
eventually
Mrs. Claus comes round too
and says, "hello, Albert," like he was a kid
because he is just a kid
always was
always is
punk as funk
and they all listen to the story of how
and why
and Albert tries very hard
very hard
not to ask too many questions
and
eventually
goes back to the dormitory
and writes stuff down
the ink disappears
into a cloud
and I wake up
in the middle of this firing range
where the bullets
are still the curse of days
and the worry
that my heart will explode
from love

and
disappointment